THE ARMY QUARTERLY SERIES

THE
NEW WARFARE

by

Brigadier C. N. BARCLAY, C.B.E., D.S.O.

GREENWOOD PRESS, PUBLISHERS
WESTPORT, CONNECTICUT

Library of Congress Cataloging in Publication Data

Barclay, Cyril Nelson, 1896-
   The new warfare.

   Reprint. Originally published: London : W. Clowes,
1953 (Army quarterly series)
   1. Psychological warfare. 2. World politics--1945-
I. Title. II. Series: Army quarterly series.
UB275.B3 1983   355.3'434   82-18375
ISBN 0-313-23793-X (lib. bdg.)

Originally published in 1953 by William Clowes and Sons, Ltd., London

Reprinted with the permission of William Clowes Publishers, Ltd.

Reprinted in 1983 by Greenwood Press
A division of Congressional Information Service, Inc.
88 Post Road West, Westport, Connecticut 06881

Printed in the United States of America

10 9 8 7 6 5 4 3 2 1

CONTENTS

Chapter		Page
	AUTHOR'S PREFACE	vii
	INTRODUCTION	ix
I.	HISTORICAL BACKGROUND	1
II.	THE PRESENT WORLD SITUATION	7
III.	THE NEW WARFARE	16
	A definition of the term	
IV.	PROPAGANDA	19
V.	UNDERGROUND ACTIVITIES	27
VI.	LIMITED "HOT WAR" AND WAR BY PROXY	33
VII.	THE ARMED ARRAY	39
VIII.	OBSTRUCTION AND PLANNED INCONVENIENCES	47
IX.	HOW WILL IT END?	53
	The Trend of World Events, and some Suggestions for Future Policy	
	EPILOGUE	65

AUTHOR'S PREFACE

MANY years ago, as a boy, I happened to be at Dover when Louis Bleriot made the first flight across the English Channel. This was regarded as a staggering feat, and I can just remember the scepticism of most of the spectators.

In 1923 I saw a picture in one of the many war books published about that time. It showed a German Cavalry Division on the march in East Prussia in 1914. The Divisional Commander—complete with monocle and a very swagger Cavalry greatcoat—was standing by the roadside, with a numerous staff, watching his troops go forward into action. It was a brave display, typifying the apparent zenith of an arm which had influenced battles and campaigns, and decided the fate of kingdoms, for centuries. A few weeks later I read that Lord Haig had given it as his opinion that horsed Cavalry would always play a part in war.

Bleriot's Channel flight was 44 years ago, the incident of the German Cavalry Division took place 39 years ago and Lord Haig made his statement 30 years ago. To-day Bleriot's successors, flying in thousands of aircraft, at speeds which soon may normally exceed that of sound, are capable of spreading death and destruction on an immense scale in any part of the world. The horsed Cavalryman has been obsolete for at least 14 years: he received his congé in the Polish Campaign of 1939.

It is at such tempo that changes, and modern developments, take place. What seems inconceivable becomes commonplace in the space of a few years. That which appears to be permanent is swept away in less than a generation.

The acceptance of new conditions is comparatively easy for the young but very difficult for the middle-aged and elderly, who tend to see permanent changes as temporary expedients and new methods as vulgar "stunts". As it is the customary order of things that we should be governed, and guided, mostly by elderly people, there is a very real danger of present-day conditions being seriously misjudged and of authoritative opinion lagging behind realities.

I cannot claim to be among the young, and hardly among the middle-aged; but for some time I have felt that the accepted view of present-day conditions, and of the future in international events, may be entirely wrong. In particular, I believe that the idea that we are experiencing an uneasy peace is mistaken. I think conditions in the 1950s are more correctly described as limited *war*—a war which *may* turn very sharply into a full-scale shooting war, but which, in my view, is more likely to persist for a long time in its present form. This is the idea which inspired this book—"The New Warfare".

I wish to emphasize that I make no claim to information not available to any member of the public, or that my contentions are any more than reasoned opinions on these very complex matters.

The book was ready for press a few days before Marshal Stalin's death and the text has been re-examined in the light of developments since then. No substantial alterations appeared to be justified and very few were made. We must be careful not to judge hastily, and not to hail a change in Soviet tactics as a change of heart and policy.

C. N. BARCLAY

Camberley
May, 1953

INTRODUCTION

In Europe to-day the rival forces of West and East face each other in full battle array. In Asia "Hot War" is in progress in Korea and Indo-China and guerrilla operations in Malaya and elsewhere. Throughout the world underground activities, and cold warfare, are being waged unceasingly. Both groups of nations are spending huge sums on arms and equipment and maintaining large conscript forces. These conditions are not due to a series of isolated incidents but conform to world-wide plans consequent on the apparently irreconcilable, and bitter, rivalry between Western Freedom and Russian Communism.

Yet, we call this peace; but to many thinking people it is more like war. They hold the view that fear of another full-scale shooting war, combined with the prospects of complete economic ruin as its aftermath, has induced the nations to invent another kind of warfare—a war of limited shooting, sometimes by proxy, and involving elaborately prepared campaigns of threats, propaganda and subversive activities.

We may call the whole process "The New Warfare", and it is the purpose of this book to examine every aspect of the conditions which the term implies.

It would seem that this theme is entirely logical. Clausewitz' famous dictum, that "war is a continuation of policy by other means", implies that nations normally attempt to gain their ends by peaceful methods and only resort to war when diplomacy fails and they think that war may be profitable. It is not unreasonable to suppose that, in certain conditions, an intermediate course of action may be adopted —something which is more militant than the usual diplomacy but does not amount to full-scale war. It is at least arguable that these conditions exist to-day—the certainty that another total war will bring disaster to all, including the victors; the instability and discontent existing among many peoples, which make them susceptible to propaganda and subversive activities; and the fact that many small groups have old scores to pay off against other small groups—all these are favourable to the prosecution of limited warfare.

INTRODUCTION

It is, of course, true that since Marshal Stalin's death we have witnessed a change in Soviet tactics. It would be foolish not to welcome the signs of cooperation, and an apparent desire for better understanding, which the new Russian leaders have made manifest recently. It would, however, be equally foolish to assume that Stalin's successors have renounced any of their basic aims and objectives. The change is in the short-term method rather than in the long-term policy. Whilst from the Democracies a responsible and sober response, in press and speech, is clearly demanded, caution and vigilance are also necessary. We must not be deceived into believing that years of abuse and hostility can be resolved by a few gestures of goodwill in matters which may seem important now, but which are comparatively trivial in the over-all World scene.

Other developments may have occurred before this book is published; but it is hardly conceivable that the two opposing ideologies of East and West can have attained more than a beginning to the solution of their difficulties. Nevertheless, it will not be out of place to express the hope that some aspects, at least, of the "New Warfare", as I have described it, will soon become history rather than activities still to be reckoned with.

The term "Communism", when used in this book, has no reference to the original meaning of the word but is used to describe the Soviet form of so-called "Communism", which is almost indistinguishable from Nazism and Fascism.

CHAPTER I

HISTORICAL BACKGROUND

IN purely technical matters a study of the past is not always helpful; but in the more conservative realm of human relations, and reactions, history often provides a good guide. Those whose business it is to consider, and influence, the wider aspects of world affairs may, with profit, examine the experiences of their predecessors. It will not, therefore, be out of place to begin this study with a glance at history and an investigation of the circumstances which have fermented wars, decided their pattern and shaped the aftermath of hostilities. It will not be necessary to delve further back than the Middle Ages, nor to consider events in great detail. If we can trace the general trend it will be sufficient for our purposes.

The student of medieval campaigns is at once struck by the small sizes of the rival forces. Although populations were, of course, much smaller, the proportion between fighters and non-fighters, in those days, was much less than in more recent times. The following are typical examples:

Battle	*Estimated Strengths*
Hastings (1066) . .	Normans—slightly less than 9,000 and the Saxons about the same.
Crécy (1346) . .	The English Army under Edward III was about 9,000, the French being estimated at about four times that number.
Agincourt (1415) . .	English about 6,000. The French have been variously estimated at between 10,000 and 200,000; but it is probable that less than 45,000 actually deployed for battle.
Towton (1461) . .	In this, the greatest battle ever fought on British soil, the rival armies consisted of approximately: Yorkists 36,000. Lancastrians 40,000.

These very small numbers give the impression that war was not taken very seriously—merely a sport between rival kings and princelings, and their retainers, for the purpose of redressing an insult or seizing a castle, a town or a strip of territory. In many cases this was so, especially in contests between minor princes and chieftains, whose warlike activities were usually kept within reasonable bounds by the "overlord" to whom most underling-rulers owed suzerainty.

In the national contests, however—such as the frequent, and at one time almost continuous, wars between England and France—there must have been other factors which limited the scale of operations. There was, at times, intense hatred between rulers and people in the rival countries, and the campaigns were usually waged with great ferocity. There is no reason for believing that there were any limits to the scale of operations, other than those imposed by the conditions of the times. We can at once discard fear of combat as a factor. Man has never shirked death, or mutilation, in battle for a cause which he considered just or to his advantage. We must seek other reasons.

In this period the bulk of the people lived a hand-to-mouth existence, often on the brink of starvation. Any considerable withdrawal of adult manhood from agriculture, or the simple crafts of the times, would have resulted in immediate want and privation. Communications were primitive in the extreme. Occasionally it was possible to use waterways as a means of transport; but, in the main, movement was confined to ill-kept roads, which were little more than cart-tracks. The only transport "vehicles" were pack animals, cumbersome carts and the fighting man himself. These conditions prevented the assembly, and maintenance, of large forces. Winter conditions of cold and flood usually resulted in the suspension of hostilities, and the rival armies either dispersed or went into "winter quarters".

The national finances of those days were very simple. There was no equivalent to our modern system of "credits", and most campaigns were paid for from the ruler's private treasure chest—which was not infrequently far from full. This, and other considerations, made any regular system of supply, comparable to that provided by our modern Lines of Communication, out of the question. The troops, and their horses, lived on the country, and as the countryside often provided only the bare necessities for the normal civil population, and was frequently uninhabited or very sparsely populated, the surplus for a field army was small.

HISTORICAL BACKGROUND

Thus the size of armies, and the scope of war, were limited in the Middle Ages mostly by *economic* causes, and these in turn limited the effect of war. Although casualties among the actual combatants were often heavy, the civil population, with the exception of those living in the actual path of combat, remained undisturbed. Moreover, the evil aftermath was usually slight and of short duration. Peace terms were not, as a rule, very severe, and within a short time the inhabitants of the theatre of operations were able to return to a normal life.

Improvements in communications, the trend towards "credit" finance, better weapons and organization, combined with rises in the general standard of life and inventiveness, gradually increased the scope and consequences of war. It is, however, true to say that no revolutionary transformation took place prior to the Napoleonic Wars of the late 18th and early 19th centuries. We then witness an abrupt change. War ceased to be a matter confined to princes, generals and soldiers, but began to assume the form of the nation in arms. There were several reasons for this, but undoubtedly the main one was Napoleon himself. He possessed a peculiar genius which enabled him to take advantage of improving conditions, which made war on a new pattern, and more extensive scale, possible. In his latter years, when he was head of the State, the whole resources of France were subordinated to his military ambitions—ambitions which it took the combined strength of the rest of Europe to thwart.

This new phase in military history resulted in much larger armies, as the following figures show:

Campaign	*Approximate Strengths*
Napoleon's invasion of Russia	The initial strength of the Grand Army was about 350,000 men.
Waterloo (1815).	Napoleon 124,000
	Wellington 93,000 ⎫
	Blücher 120,000 ⎬ 213,000

In addition, England, France and other powers maintained considerable Naval forces.

The cost of military equipment had also risen sharply. Guns, muskets, ammunition and transport were vastly more expensive than the equipments of the Middle Ages. Moreover, the increased numbers of men and animals were no longer able to live on the country: much of an army's requirements had to be met by a regular system of supply—the forerunner of our present elaborate supply services and Lines of Communications. Improved methods of agriculture, better manufacturing methods, better organization and more orderly financial systems enabled the nations to support war on this scale to an extent which would have been impossible 300 years before. Nevertheless, the strain was very severe for the whole of Europe, and the evil economic effects of the Napoleonic Wars lasted for many years after Waterloo. Against this was the fact that wars were still localized, not world-wide. The countries of Europe, and Russia, were the only victims.

It can be said that by 1815 many years of almost continuous war had thrown Europe off her balance but had not brought the prolonged instability, hatreds and general havoc which we know to-day. The world had seriously stretched its economy but had not paralysed it.

The next era of military advancement saw the rise of Prussia, terminating in the Franco-Prussian War of 1870–71. By then the advent of railways, improved roads, greater industrial power, and the organization of Germany for war by the Bismarck–Moltke combination, made possible the employment of ever larger armies and induced much greater speed and flexibility in battle. The following figures for the 1870–71 War give some idea of these increases:

Germans	518,000 men	
	1,584 guns	
French	270,000 men	on mobilization
	925 guns	
	plus	
	120,000 men	MacMahon's Army (mostly *Gardes Mobiles*)
	324 guns	formed later at Châlons.

This era did not, however, place any serious strain on world, or European, economy. German superiority in military technique prevented a long-drawn-out struggle, and the peace terms imposed on France, considered severe at the time, were not crushing. Indeed, the indemnity of 5,000 million francs (about £200,000,000), seems a trifling sum to-day, and was, in fact, paid off very quickly— by September, 1873.

The Franco-Prussian War was the last large-scale war to remain

HISTORICAL BACKGROUND

localized, and the last to be waged within the compass of the economy of the times.* The 75 years which follow witnessed two World Wars which not only brought widespread slaughter and destruction on an unparalleled scale, at the time, but have left an aftermath of chaos, hatred and misery, which, judged by present indications, may continue for generations.

The Great War of 1914–18 was the first to be financed under the complex "credits" system of modern times. This system gave an exaggerated view of the world's capacity to support a prolonged total war. For more than 4 years practically the whole of Europe spent its energy in scientific slaughter, in destroying its capital assets and in producing war material only to blow it to pieces. In the latter years the United States of America was similarly engaged on a considerable scale.

At its peak the 1914–18 War was costing Britain more than £5,000,000 per day. The cost of the shells in the opening bombardment of a single battle (the Battle of Messines, in May, 1917) amounted to £17,500,000. In the United Kingdom alone 25,510 guns were manufactured for the Army, 1,040 war vessels were built after the outbreak of war and 55,093 aircraft constructed. In the Battle of the Somme, in 1916, both sides suffered approximately 600,000 casualties and the total losses in dead during the whole war were: Britain, 996,230; France, over 1,000,000; Germany, "official" figure, over 2,000,000, but later calculations nearly double this.†

With singularly little foresight, and remarkable lack of judgment, the statesmen of the world failed to appreciate that, after more than four years of slaughter and destruction on this scale, recovery would not be a matter of a few years but would take several decades.

The League of Nations was initiated mainly for the purpose of preserving peace; but as the U.S.A. was not a member, and it had no means of enforcing its decisions, it failed singularly in its purpose.

Before the world had fully recovered from the 1914–18 War the Second World War was upon us. This, lasting as it did for nearly 6 years, and involving Europe and much of Asia and America in a full-scale effort, had an even more disastrous effect on world affairs than the previous contest. The increased costs of war material and the greater destructive power of modern weapons—particularly bomber

---

* The Russo-Japanese War is excluded as it was conducted in a remote part of Asia and was not a death struggle for either combatant.

† Most of the figures given in this paragraph have been taken from *A Short History of World War I*, by Brigadier-General Sir James E. Edmonds.

aircraft—disturbed world economy to a much greater extent than in 1914–18* and have left an aftermath of economic ruin which seems almost irreparable.

From the foregoing paragraphs three fundamental facts emerge, which it will be profitable to tabulate clearly and remember:

Firstly. Up to the middle of the 18th century war had been restricted to a comparatively small proportion of the nation, and the simple weapons and equipments could be provided without imposing undue strain on national economy.

Secondly. From the end of the 18th century until 1914 we see an era in which war had become a much more serious, and disturbing, business. Nevertheless, wars remained localized, and although the burden had increased, and the aftermath become more serious, the effect was not crushing.

Thirdly. The two Great Wars of this century were totally different in character from all previous contests. They were world-wide in scope and they were ruinous to the complicated international economy which we had evolved.

It can be said that, up to 1914, man waged war on a scale he could afford. Since 1914 he has waged it on a scale which is beyond his means.

This is the background from which we can view events to-day.

* During the peak period of the Second World War Britain was spending more than £9,000,000 per day and the U.S.A. about £16,000,000 per day.

CHAPTER II

THE PRESENT WORLD SITUATION

THE ROOT CAUSE

BEFORE attempting to assess the present world situation it will be as well to examine the root cause of our troubles, the hostility between the two ideologies of East and West—Russian Communism and Free Democracy.

That of the West is based fundamentally on the old religions, of which Christianity is the most important, but in which others, owing allegiance to a spiritual God, or Gods—such as the Jewish, Mohammedan and Hindu religions—are also conspicuous. The modern expression of this ideology is the Democratic State, with its elected parliamentary form of government and its free institutions.

Russian Communism is quite different. It is based not on a Deity but on the deification of Man himself, who is regarded as the be-all and end-all of everything. This creed is expressed in the Totalitarian form of government, in which the destinies of all are in the hands of a few, and in which every individual is dedicated to an all-powerful State, to be sent here or there according to requirements and without any regard to his, or her, own wishes. In practice there is little difference between Russian Communism and the Nazi and Fascist creeds of Germany and Italy.

A main cause of cleavage is that, whereas Western Democracy admits the right of all peoples to live under any form of government they choose, Communism is dedicated to spreading its tenets far and wide and irrespective of the wishes of those whom it strives to engulf. Its aim is World Communism, by any means. This fundamental difference gives the Soviet a pronounced advantage in furthering its policy. Those who aspire to attain something are invariably more enthusiastic, and more ruthless, than those who merely attempt to prevent something happening. In military parlance Communism, by the very nature of its doctrine, *vis-à-vis* Democracy, holds the initiative.

These preliminary remarks, whilst giving a brief generalization of the differences between Western Democracy and Eastern Communism, should not create the impression that the dividing line is a clear-cut one. Many Democratic countries—such as France, Italy and the Scandinavian countries—have considerable numbers of Communist adherents, and even the bitterest opponents of the Soviet system—America and Britain—are not free from subversive elements—elements which often influence affairs to a degree out of all proportion to their numbers. Similarly, in Russia, and more particularly in the Satellite countries, there are people, numbered probably in millions, who detest Communism and in their hearts still favour Christianity or one of the other ancient religions. Their voices are not heard, however, as open opposition is ruthlessly suppressed. Here, again, we see conditions which appear to operate against Democracy, which tolerates Communism in its midst, whilst its opponents suppress contrary views. It may be, however, that this is not such a disadvantage as it seems. An enemy in the open, whose members can be counted, is less dangerous than one forced to operate in the dark, and whose strength is problematical.

It might be thought that the world is large enough to support both ideologies without the one trespassing on the other. It is possible to draw a line round the globe which divides the two groups very "tidily", and each possesses a self-sufficient economy. This would not be an ideal solution; but it would be reasonably satisfactory, and certainly preferable to present conditions. On closer investigation, however, it becomes apparent that no such simple solution is possible at present; but the idea has possibilities. The chief obstacle is the Soviets' missionary tactics, which seem inseparable from Communism—the passion to convert the whole world, whatever the difficulties and cost. To some it is questionable, however, if the West can ever be acquiescent, whilst many Communist methods and customs remain so repugnant to Western ideals. The mass trials, the forced confessions, the periodical purges and shootings, the labour camps, the persecution of religion, the secret police—these are things which many in the Democracies feel cannot be tolerated in silence, anywhere.

It would, however, be foolish to argue that everything about Communism is bad, and everything connected with Western Democracy is good. Exaggerated praise for a cause, and exaggerated abuse of an opponent, are sure ways of weakening an argument. In most matters, such as our faith and our politics, we must select that which conforms most closely to our views. We cannot hope to find one with which we agree in every detail. Communism has some characteristics which we can applaud—an apparent absence of corruption in the

THE PRESENT WORLD SITUATION

financial sense, and the spirit of service and enthusiasm engendered among the genuine members of the party. We can also detect certain defects in the Democratic system: the unedifying vote-catching of party politics; the apathy towards the Christian religion which most Democratic States profess to embrace; and the occasional exposures of corruption in such matters as tax-evasion and the handling of public funds and contracts.

Nevertheless, it is a marked characteristic of relations between the two ideologies that there is little compromise. There are very few waverers. One is either an out-and-out Communist who hates Democracy, or a member of the Free World who regards Communism as an invention of the devil.

Fundamental Facts

Out of this root cause of all our trouble a few fundamental facts emerge, and a short examination of these is the next step towards an understanding of the concrete problems which now confront us. They may be summarized as follows:

(a) *Communism and Democracy appear to be irreconcilably opposed and fairly evenly matched physically.*

This suggests that the antagonism between the two groups will exist for a very long time.

(b) *World economy is very seriously strained. Many are starving and even the most prosperous have had to forgo some luxuries and some things previously regarded as necessities.*

This indicates that the present "New Warfare" is the limit which the nations can wage without disaster to all. As far as we can judge, a full-scale shooting war, with atomic weapons, would deal mankind a blow from which it could not recover. Organized society, in both East and West, would be irretrievably ruined.

(c) *The present high cost of armaments places a ruinous load on both groups and is the main obstacle to an improvement in economic conditions. Yet neither side dares to relax in this respect.*

This seems to point to a continuance of the conditions given in (b), which suggest that a shooting war is not likely.

(d) *Both groups possess the men, the equipment, the organization and the military technique to start a full-scale war at a moment's notice.*

In the view of many this condition makes war almost inevitable, sooner or later. They find no precedent for vast armaments not resulting, eventually, in war. Nevertheless, there are indications that this opinion may be wrong. The condition has lasted for seven years without a major clash, and the world has now grown less sensitive to minor incidents. A frontier clash, an open insult, an arrest, a trial or a shooting, which at one time would have caused acute indignation followed by an ultimatum, are now regarded as mere day-to-day incidents in a world which has lost its manners and become toughened by wars, and armed peace, over a period of nearly 40 years. Moreover, the major weapons of a future war—the atom bomb and other nuclear missiles—are not in the hands of troops who might use them prematurely. They are what might be termed strategic, or long-range, weapons and, as yet, few in number. The decision to use them will be a carefully calculated one at the highest level—a factor which mitigates against an accidental, or ill-considered, opening of hostilities.

THE CONCRETE PROBLEMS WHICH HAVE DEVELOPED SINCE 1945

The next stage is to trace developments which have led up to the world situation which faces us to-day.

On the 7th May, 1945, Germany surrendered unconditionally, and 3 months later, on the 14th August, Japan followed suit. The Allies—headed by America, the British Commonwealth and Russia—were thus undisputed masters of the world, with their late enemies in ruins and at their mercy.

After 4 years and 3 months of total war a quarter of a century before, and 6 years of similar hostilities only just completed, mankind seemed overdue for a long respite, if not perpetual peace. No sensible person expected that the task would be an easy one, or that recovery would be rapid. Nevertheless, it was reasonable to suppose that the powers had learnt something from their experiences, and that all would make a genuine effort to cooperate for peace and the rehabilitation of our ruined economy. With this end in view the United Nations Organization (U.N.O.) was set up, with the main

THE PRESENT WORLD SITUATION

task of securing peace and goodwill among the Nations—not, as in the case of the old League of Nations, without the cooperation of the U.S.A., but embracing practically the whole world.

Towards the end of the war a new scientific means of destruction had been demonstrated. On the 5th August, 1945, an American aircraft dropped the first atom bomb on Hiroshima, followed by a second on Nagasaki on the 9th August. These bombs caused death and destruction on an unprecedented scale and left a serious radio-active aftermath for many days. It was clear that any nation, or group, possessing a monopoly of such weapons was unassailable and, if aggressively inclined, a potential danger to the rest of the world. This monopoly was enjoyed by the U.S.A. until September, 1949, when the American President disclosed that his Government had evidence that an atomic explosion had occurred in Russia. Since then (on 3rd October, 1952), a British A-bomb has been detonated at Monte Bello Island, off Australia.

This revolutionary invention has influenced post-war world affairs in two directions. It is fundamental to a study of our problem that these be clearly understood.

The restraining influence on Russia

Unfortunately the high hopes of peace, and mutual cooperation among nations, were soon dispelled. Almost as soon as the last shot of World War II had been fired Russia, supported by her Communist Satellites, began to show an aggressive trend and open hostility towards her former Allies. It seems probable that *her ambitions were kept in check only by the realization that America possessed the atom bomb and, in certain eventualities, was prepared to use it.*

The aspect of uncertainty

There is every indication that developments in nuclear weapons will be rapid. Since the first Russian detonation in 1949 (followed by another in 1951) Britain has shown her ability to manufacture atom bombs, and America has exploded a hydrogen bomb, said to be many times more powerful than any atom bomb. We also know that progress is not confined to bombs, but that tactical missiles of many kinds, with an atomic charge, already exist. It is evident that we have reached a stage in which conventional weapons, with a lethal effect measured in yards, are being replaced, or at least augmented, by weapons of obliteration which will result in death and destruction for miles from the point of detonation and leave a radio-active aftermath lasting for days, perhaps weeks. Moreover, these weapons are now in the hands of both potentially belligerent groups. It is probable that America still retains a substantial lead; but this is not certain. *The uncertainty of the potentialities of this terrible new weapon, and the uncertainty in one camp of developments in the other, are very potent factors in restraining action likely to bring about another full-scale shooting war.*

Bearing these two factors in mind it will now be convenient to consider the circumstances in the international field when hostilities ended in 1945 and to trace developments up to the present time.

With the collapse of Germany and Japan all thoughts in the Western countries, headed by America, the British Commonwealth and France, turned towards demobilization and rehabilitation. Their main purpose was to reduce their armed forces to the minimum and get busy with the task of restoring the ravages of the past 6 years. Housing, education, an even economy and improved social services, together with a return to peace-time industry and expanding trade facilities—these were the matters uppermost in all minds.

In the Soviet Union—or rather among the small band of leaders who controlled its destinies—the outlook was quite different. Their war partnership with the Western Democracies had been one of expedience and convenience. They had no love for their Allies and no sympathy with their aims or way of life. Whereas the Western Allies had regarded the defeat of Germany and Japan as the aim and ultimate goal, Russia regarded the victorious conclusion of the war as merely a stepping-stone towards the attainment of something more—World Communism. There can be little doubt that, but for Allied monopoly in the atomic weapon and the demonstrations of its terrible effects at Hiroshima and Nagasaki, Russia would have adopted a much more militant attitude and pressed her claims more closely. In the years 1946 to 1948 there was little to prevent Russia marching into France, Greece and many other countries, and occupying most of Europe—except the threat of the atom bomb.

This restraining influence continued until the autumn of 1949, when the detonation of the first Russian atom bomb showed the two groups to be nearer parity—although how near it is impossible to say. This completely changed the situation, but left the consequences much the same. Prior to this, restraint had been imposed by Russian fear of the American monopoly in nuclear weapons. Now it was imposed by fear of the consequences of an all-out atomic war, and uncertainty as to the outcome. No nation takes the initiative to bring about a shooting war unless it thinks it can win, and win quickly. The new, and almost untried, weapon makes accurate assessment very difficult. In 1914 and 1939 Germany had reasonable grounds for believing that the odds were in her favour, and on both occasions she was eventually defeated. With these examples it is small wonder that the nations shrink from taking the plunge in the atomic age, in which accurate speculation on the effects, and outcome, of war is even more difficult.

The two atom bombs dropped on Japan must have come as an unpleasant shock to the Kremlin. The situation which the Soviet had hoped for at the end of 1945 was one in which Anglo-American forces were hotly engaged with Japan, who was still resisting stoutly. In Europe the weary nations would be demobilizing rapidly and, after years of Nazi occupation, would be ripe for Communism. The Soviet forces, to be retained on a war footing, would have little difficulty in dominating the whole of Europe. This was, no doubt, the picture; but it was all upset by the atom bomb—which brought the war in the East to an abrupt end, and tipped the balance of armed power in favour of America and the Free World.

The Soviet leaders were not slow to appreciate that the changed conditions demanded new methods. There must be a show at cooperation, and a more stealthy approach to the problems which they had hoped to solve by force, or the threat of force.

The Russians were practised hands at "Cold Warfare". In 1939, after partitioning Poland with Germany, they had virtually annexed Esthonia, Latvia and Lithuania, by the process known as "Mutual Assistance Pacts". Later they were to absorb the whole of Poland, East Prussia, Eastern Germany, Czechoslovakia and other countries. Finally, the victory of the Chinese Communists resulted in a large slice of Asia becoming Moscow-controlled.

In carrying out this policy the Kremlin leaders were not without guidance. Between 1933 and 1939 Herr Hitler had obtained control of large areas of Europe by "Cold Warfare" methods and without firing a shot. The underground activities of Soviet agents, and sympathizers, followed the Nazi "fifth column" pattern with which we had become familiar in the early days of war.

It soon became apparent, however, that the methods of Hitler were not entirely suited to Russian needs. Nazi Germany's successes were obtained at the expense of small countries—Austria and Czechoslovakia. Clearly something much more cunning and comprehensive was required if Russia was to be successful against the full array of the Free World. With typical Eastern patience she set in motion a long-term policy based on threats, subversive activities, propaganda and limited or proxy war—designed to avoid the hazards and crippling economic effects of open hostilities on the 1914-18 and 1939-45 scale.

Against this policy the Western Democracies have been on the defensive for 7 years, with all the disadvantages of a defensive attitude.

The Situation To-day

At the present time (1953) the situation may be summarized as follows:

Geographical Division

The Free World	The Communist World
West Europe	The U.S.S.R.
Scandinavia	Eastern Europe, with the exception of Greece and Turkey
Greece	
Turkey	
India, Pakistan and most of South-East Asia and the Middle East	China
Africa	*Note:*—Although Communist, Yugoslavia has broken with the Soviet and inclines towards friendly relations with the West.
Australia	
New Zealand	
The American Continent.	

Penetration

In many countries of the Free World—France, Italy, India and others—Communism has made serious penetrations. No doubt the converse also applies and many behind the Iron Curtain are opposed to Communism; but their numbers are difficult to judge, as they are either inactive or forced to work underground.

Hot War

In Asia (Korea, Indo-China and Malaya) the Soviet is conducting limited war by proxy.

Armaments

Both groups are very heavily armed and in many places—North-West Europe, Hong Kong, etc.—the rival forces face each other in full battle array, ready for instant action.

THE PRESENT WORLD SITUATION

Political Relations

Almost daily—in the press, over the radio, by normal diplomatic channels or in the Councils of the United Nations—an accusation or threat is made, or an insult hurled, which 50 years ago would have resulted in an ultimatum, mobilization and troop movements and probably war.

Thus we have conditions which are not war according to the old conceptions; but which can hardly be called peace. Mankind—conscious of the terrible, and certain, consequences of another shooting war—has been forced to other methods of conducting hostilities—a war of limited and proxy fighting, threats, propaganda and subversive activities—the only kind of war it is capable of undertaking without bringing the whole world to ruin.

In this situation the Soviet and her Satellites gain some advantage from their low standard of living, compared with the West. They have mostly never known anything but harsh social and economic conditions.

It would seem that this state of affairs may last for a very considerable time. Its cost is just within the compass of world economy, fear will prevent its extension to a shooting war, and the rivalry between the two groups is so intense as to preclude the likelihood of any rapid improvement in their relations. In view of the bitter hostility which has existed for so long it is hardly credible that the friendly gestures from the Soviet since Marshal Stalin's death—even assuming that they reflect a genuine desire for better relations—can be more than the first few strides along the tortuous road to real peace.

CHAPTER III

THE NEW WARFARE

A Definition of the Term

The term "Cold Warfare" is in common use to describe the hostile methods now employed in world affairs. Various attempts have been made to define the term, of which the following is perhaps the most authoritative:

> "The policy of making mischief by all methods short of war—that is to say, short of war involving the Soviet Union in open hostilities."*

This definition may have been adequate at the time it was drafted; but in the conditions which have developed since 1950 it is open to criticism. The word "mischief" is altogether too mild—savouring of school-boy escapades—to describe the serious incidents and events which now characterize the hostility between East and West. Moreover, the last sentence gives the impression that "Cold Warfare" is, and must remain, a monopoly of the Soviet Union. It is true that hitherto this view has been almost unanimously accepted in the Democracies; but if it persists the inevitable result will be to give Russia the permanent initiative in a struggle in which the defeat of the Free World cannot be contemplated. Only a few months ago Field-Marshal Lord Montgomery emphasized that "Cold Warfare" is a serious issue, to be won or lost, and that if we wish to win we must fight it with no less skill and determination than we fought the shooting war.

It is, however, apparent that, under the definition given above, the term "Cold Warfare" includes only some, and not all, of the activities and long-term plans which unhappily divide the world. The term "The New Warfare" is considered better, and more comprehensive.

In this chapter an attempt is made to explain, in general terms, the expression "The New Warfare".

The term can be considered under five headings:

---

* This definition is the one given in *Defence in the Cold War*, compiled by a Study Group of the Royal Institute of International Affairs, published in 1950.

(1) *Propaganda*

The process by which one's own people are confirmed in the righteousness of their cause, the efficiency of their leaders and the evil intentions of their opponents, whilst one's enemies are so saturated with arguments that they begin to doubt the wisdom of their own creed and eventually, it is hoped, become sympathetic to their country's enemies and traitors to their own State.

The mediums employed are: direct contact by propaganda agents; by radio broadcasts; in the press; and by means of spurious international meetings of industrialists, trade union officials, scientists etc., and the so-called "Peace Meetings" with which we have become familiar.

Underground War, Sabotage, Intimidation and Bribes

In its extreme form this may involve a complete underground organization aimed at the overthrow of a government and the absorption of the country as a Satellite, such as was done in Czechoslovakia in 1948. More often it is on a less ambitious scale—the fermenting of strikes, sabotage in factories and ordinary espionage—but invariably designed to bring about eventual subjugation.

(3) *War by Proxy on a Limited Scale*

There are several examples of this, in varying degrees. At the top of the scale are Korea, and Indo-China, where full-scale wars, involving considerable forces, are involved. In Malaya small-scale, but nevertheless exhausting, operations have been going on for years. All have one factor in common: they absorb large numbers of Western servicemen, and an immense amount of equipment, without the employment of a single Russian fighting man, and very little Russian equipment. Soviet participation is almost entirely confined to advice and encouragement.

In this category comes the encouragement of civil war, whenever there is a good chance of a victory. By this means the immense population, and material resources, of China have been won for Communism.

(4) *The Armed Threat*

Overshadowing all other activities are the immense Naval, Land and Air Forces, with their powerful conventional weapons now, or about to be, augmented by atomic missiles. These large forces serve two purposes. They can be used by an aggressor to threaten and coerce, and they also provide a measure of insurance, available as a last resort if "New Warfare" methods fail and, despite all, a shooting war begins.

(5) *Obstruction and Planned Mischief*

Examples of these are legion—the isolation of Berlin by closing roads, inspecting incoming and outgoing vehicles, etc.; arrests on the West–East German frontier; excessive use of the veto on the Security Council of U.N.O., etc.

We are now in a position to be more explicit regarding the term "New Warfare", which may be defined as:

"The means by which a nation (or group of nations) seeks to impose its will on others, by all means short of total war, and without disturbing its own economy to an extent which is unbearable, or unacceptable, to its people. The methods include: propaganda, obstruction, planned mischief, underground war, sabotage, intimidation, bribes, armed threats, limited war and war by proxy."

A peculiar, and indeed remarkable, feature of this warfare up-to-date is the one-sided character of certain aspects of the conflict. What has hitherto been called "Cold Warfare" has been assumed to be the exclusive monopoly of the Soviet—a form of hostility which the Democracies are prepared to parry, but disdain to practise. The "Hot War" in Korea, and elsewhere, they understand and fight, as best they can, on equal terms. This difference of view towards different aspects of the same problem is undoubtedly due to the use of the two terms "Cold War" and "Hot War", which convey the impression of two unconnected activities. This alone is sufficient reason for including *all* aspects of the problem within the single term "*The New Warfare*"—warfare which we must plan, coordinate and conduct to win by superior methods, better organization and greater determination than our opponents.

CHAPTER IV

PROPAGANDA

A WELL-KNOWN English dictionary defines propaganda as:

"Any concerted action for the spread of opinions and principles: action done, statement made, purely for the purpose of inculcating an idea or belief."

There is nothing new in this. Ministers of religion, politicians, Trade Union officials, the proprietors of Pears Soap and Guinness's Stout, the designers of posters advocating a holiday at So-and-So-on-Sea, all practise the art. In fact there is hardly anybody who leads an active life who does not practise propaganda, or come under its influence, almost daily. What is new is the scope and ingenuity with which it is now used in International Affairs, on a world-wide scale, by methods which modern inventions have made possible.

When we speak of propaganda to-day we do not mean the ordinary methods of advertising and advocacy but the highly organized systems of mass persuasion as practised by the late Doctor Goebbels, and the Soviet authorities, for war or political purposes on an International scale.

Propaganda in the International sense comes under three headings:

(*a*) For home consumption.
(*b*) For enemy, or potential enemy, consumption.
(*c*) For the consumption of neutrals or "waverers".

For Home Consumption

In times of stress governments often find it necessary to stimulate the nerves, courage and faith of their nationals by carefully planned propaganda. The more excitable and temperamental the people, the less homogeneous they are, and the greater their trials and tribulations, the greater the need for propaganda to sustain them. The British have never found it necessary to employ this kind of propaganda very extensively. By nature they thrive on adversity (such as in 1940, after Dunkirk), they are not a temperamental people and, on the whole, are very poor subjects for propaganda of any sort.

On the other hand our late enemies evolved the most elaborate system, under the direction of Doctor Goebbels, for home and hostile consumption. This organization, although ridiculed by our counter-propaganda, was undoubtedly very effective *within* the Reich and did much to sustain the high morale and discipline maintained by German troops and civilians till the end.

Soviet efforts are devoted mainly to this class of propaganda, by exalting and reiterating the Communist creed. In this they are very successful; although, by driving their internal opponents underground, it may be that they appear to be more successful than is actually the case. Moreover, the low standard of education and intelligence in many parts of the Soviet Union, and her Satellites, makes the task a fairly easy one. It is also very necessary in a country consisting of so many diverse races and creeds and with appended Satellite States.

Some forms of Russian propaganda for internal consumption seem to us elementary and clumsy and hardly credible among even the most gullible people. Stories that Russia defeated Germany in the late war single handed, that she played a leading part in the defeat of Japan (whom she hardly fought at all), that Russian scientists and technicians invented all kinds of things in which they actually had no hand whatever, the story of American use of germ warfare in Korea—these seem so fantastic as to run the risk of defeating their object, by exposing the whole system for the fraud which it is. It must be remembered, however, that this propaganda is put out for people who have never known the benefits of a free press, freedom to listen to foreign radio broadcasts, or Western education, and who live under the shadow of the informer and the secret police. The Soviet Government is their only source of information. Among these, propaganda which to us appears ridiculous, may be very effective.

It may be argued that this does not explain how a man like the Dean of Canterbury can be successfully won to Communism. Such cases are, however, very exceptional. In a country of 50 million people there are always a few well-educated people with a mental make-up which can be made to believe anything. Most of our own Communists are either ignorant or disgruntled, or inspired by selfish motives.

For Enemy, or Potential Enemy, Consumption

This is a much more intricate form of propaganda than that for home consumption, and to be effective requires great subtlety and a high standard of technique. It is obviously more difficult to hoodwink foreigners, whose susceptibilities are imperfectly understood, than one's own people. Moreover, the effect of propaganda for home consumption can be quickly, and accurately, estimated and, if not satisfactory, altered at short notice. The effect of that abroad is much more difficult to judge, and more difficult to adjust if it proves unsatisfactory. Home propaganda is not usually countered by efficient, if by any, methods; whereas every virile country is at pains to counter the propaganda of its enemies.

In the immediate pre-war years German propaganda earned a reputation to which it was hardly entitled. The successes in Austria, Czechoslovakia and elsewhere were attributed to its excellence, but on examination this contention cannot be sustained. The ease with which these annexations were made was due to fear—fear of Germany's armed might, against which the rest of Europe seemed powerless—rather than to propaganda. German successes against France were, however, largely attributable to this cause, as the pre-war pacifism among sections of Frenchmen, and their lack of the "will to win" in 1940, were, at least, partly due to the influence of German propaganda. In Britain their reward was negligible, either before or during the war; and at an early stage they gave up all serious attempts to undermine this country by means of propaganda.

Since 1945 Russia has conducted an overseas propaganda campaign on a scale which far exceeds any previous attempts. She had made an intensive study of the subject, had considerable experience within her own borders and, when hostilities ended, found a world peculiarly receptive to propaganda based on promises of better things to come, and with many countries so disorganized as to be incapable of providing effective counter-measures.

Soviet propaganda has the advantage of being based on something positive—the Communist creed—which like some religions gives its adherents a loyalty in addition to, and in many cases in opposition to, loyalty to their country. As in the Middle Ages men often obeyed a Papal decree, in preference to the law of their State, so in recent times we find the ardent Communist has been a better servant to Marshal Stalin than to the country of his birth, or adoption. There has been much talk in all countries of the benefits to be derived from closer cooperation between nations and the value of an international, rather than a national outlook. It was to further these ideas that we set up The United Nations Organization. This has produced in most countries a body of well-educated men and women with a pronounced international bias. Among these, World Communism, cleverly disguised, sometimes appears to be the only virile international creed, and this is the reason for the surprising deflections to Communism from among the intellectuals of the Free World. The Democracies have nothing to offer which is as positive, or compelling, as Communism. Our religions—even where we practise them seriously—make poor propaganda, as there are so many of them and, if anything, their multiplicity tends to disunite rather than unite. Our free way of life is not sufficient, mainly because we have enjoyed it for so long that we fail to recognize its worth.

It is as well to be candid in these matters, and it is not untrue to say that the Free World is hanging on to something whose worth they do not appreciate, and which is based on a number of religions, to which many give only lip-service and which have from time to time been as bitterly opposed to each other as are East and West to-day. The propaganda of the West is at a distinct disadvantage when dealing with ill-educated, and poorly informed, masses who are constantly bombarded by the simple and positive creed of World Communism.

For Neutral Consumption

In a shooting war, propaganda for the consumption of neutral countries is a very important matter. If successful it leads, at best, to neutrals joining you as fighting Allies, and at worst to benevolent neutrality, which may be nearly as valuable. This is a form of propaganda at which the Germans were not very apt. They may have overawed some by displaying their armed might; but they were not very successful, in either of the World Wars, in persuading neutrals of the justice of their cause or the desirability of fighting as an ally of Germany.

To-day there are very few genuine neutrals. Practically the whole world has taken sides and, as far as Europe is concerned, this is expressed in the Satellite States who obsequiously follow Moscow, and the Free World members of N.A.T.O. There are, however, a number of small States, geographically ill-positioned *vis-à-vis* Russia and with a considerable Communist following in their midst. Norway, Sweden and Denmark in the north, and Greece in the Balkans, are among these.

These countries are the targets for continuous Soviet propaganda, and in the immediate post-war years their position was a very dangerous one. Now they are all members of N.A.T.O., and any coercive measures against them would give them the support of the full N.A.T.O. array, even to the extent of a shooting war—which it seems likely the Soviet, as much as the Free World, wishes to avoid.

In Europe, Switzerland is the traditional neutral, followed closely by Spain—not because she is not bitterly hostile to Communism, but because the Democracies have, until a short time ago, given her the cold shoulder. In South America, remote parts of Asia and the Pacific there are some countries which might be termed neutrals—to the extent that, owing to their geographical locations, they do not play a prominent part against Communism. They are not subject to the intense propaganda to which we are accustomed in Europe; but we may be sure they have not escaped notice and are not being neglected in the longer-term plans.

The Tactics of Propaganda for Export

British propaganda differs from that of many other countries, in that it is based on the principle of truth. Its object is to display the facts in the most favourable light. It does not countenance lies or misleading statements. We may hope that this policy is followed for ethical reasons; but it has been proved to the hilt that it is also good tactics. To be effective a propaganda machine must build up a high reputation for accuracy. Once it comes under suspicion its value among intelligent people is lost. The propaganda of the war-time regimes in Germany and Italy, and of the Soviet to-day, may be suitable for home consumption; but was, and is, so palpably untrue that the merest simpleton could hardly be deceived. Thus, alien propaganda which is written, broadcast on the radio and disseminated in public speeches has little effect on British people, or on those of other countries where the general standard of education, and acumen, is high.

It may be as well here to emphasize the obvious—that the circulation of truthful propaganda presupposes that you have some true facts which are likely to appeal to those whom you aspire to influence. The absence of this condition may account for the poor quality of some of the propaganda of this kind which comes from the East.

It would, however, be a great mistake to belittle the influence of Soviet propaganda. Communism has many adherents in France, Italy, India and Japan and a small hard-core in our own, and other, countries regarded as the bastions of Democracy. By what means, then, is the gospel spread? Undoubtedly the most common—indeed probably the only means against our own countrymen which produces any serious effect—is the direct approach. The Soviet has been at great pains to establish Communist cells in all countries, and in this policy they have been greatly assisted by the disturbance in populations brought about by the war, which has resulted in Stateless and Displaced Persons seeking asylum in all countries of the Free World, without any reciprocal measures by Russia or her Satellites. The large number of refugees crossing daily from East to West Germany is only one example of the ease with which subversive persons can be "planted" in the Democratic countries. Many of these people are not genuine refugees. Some are engaged in ordinary espionage—the uncovering of political, military and industrial secrets—and a number are propaganda agents. These are directed from Moscow and recent disclosures in France, Australia and Malaya show that special emphasis is placed on the importance of gaining control of Trade Unions, Youth Movements and similar organizations. As far as the rank and file of British Trade Unionists are concerned the majority are probably impervious to Communist propaganda. They are, however, somewhat apathetic in Union matters, and this gives the Communists a degree of control, and influence, which is out of all proportion to their numbers. It is not an uncommon experience at meetings—including meetings for the election of officials—for a 100 per cent attendance of Communists and perhaps 10 or 15 per cent of non-Communist members. This often results in the appointment of Communist officials in a Union in which non-Communists are in an overwhelming majority; but they just cannot be bothered to turn out and vote.*

Communist propaganda successes are by no means confined to the wage-earning classes. In our own country, and in Canada and America, we have experience of leading scientists and civil servants falling under its spell and, in some cases, working against their own country for the benefit of the Soviet. This appears, at first sight, to be one of the most remarkable aspects of present-day conditions; but when considering these deflections it must be remembered that in many cases those concerned were not living and working in the country of their birth, but in one of adoption. It must also be appreciated that scientists, in common with other highly specialized technicians, often lead very restricted lives. They are not always

* Anyone having doubts as to the effectiveness, and methods, of direct approach propaganda, and subversive activities, should read *The Communist Technique in Britain*, by Bob Darke—himself an ex-member of the British Communist party— (Collins, 10s. 6d.).

men of the world and are, in consequence, more gullible than those in most occupations. By reason of their work they are peculiarly susceptible to an outlook which is international, rather than national.

We can summarize the examination made in this chapter as follows:

Communist Propaganda
- (*a*) The most effective form of propaganda is that for home consumption, particularly among the youth of Satellite countries.
- (*b*) The influence of Communist propaganda in the Free World by means of radio broadcasts, and the press, is probably small. Those who listen to or read it are among the better educated and are not usually seriously affected. It does not reach the less educated, who might be influenced.
- (*c*) The most serious form of exported Communist propaganda is the direct approach—by Communist agents, or cells, directed at Trade Unions, Youth Organizations and groups of Intellectuals. This seeks, through the enthusiasm of a few converts, to gain control over the majority, who are too frequently apathetic. These tactics are particularly dangerous in undeveloped countries, which have recently been given a measure of responsible government, or whose Trade Union organization is in embryo. Nigeria and Malaya are examples. Another form of direct-approach propaganda is the meetings —sometimes in Russia, sometimes elsewhere—to which representatives of both sides of industry, politicians, students, scientists and other professional men are invited under the guise of furthering peace or their particular interests, but which are, in fact, organized to further Communist aims.

Democratic Propaganda
- (*d*) It would seem that anti-Communist propaganda for the purpose of influencing people inside Russia has little chance of achieving spectacular, or immediate, results, although some success may be expected on a long-term basis. It is very difficult to "get at" the masses in countries where reading foreign literature and listening to foreign broadcasts are illegal and where foreigners who gain legal entry are under strict supervision and constantly watched by the secret police.

(e) The Satellite countries would appear to offer better chances of success. One of these, Yugoslavia, has already rid herself of Soviet control and, although still a Communist State, is one with whom we can talk, and who shows some desire to compromise with Western ideas. Others, such as China and Poland, must still have bitter opponents of Communism in sufficient numbers to warrant the attention of Democratic propaganda.

(f) Another fruitful avenue is the countering of Communist propaganda in those countries which are on the verge of the Iron Curtain and which the Soviet strives to bring within the Communist fold. More intensive propaganda among the Communist minorities in democratic countries would also appear to be indicated.

It would seem that in this branch of "The New Warfare" the Democracies might well follow some of the principles of "Shooting Warfare". Among these are the establishment of a firm base, by directing propaganda against subversive elements in their own vital areas and by assuming a propaganda offensive—not against the impregnable bastions of Communism, but against the "soft spots".

CHAPTER V

UNDERGROUND ACTIVITIES

THE dividing line between the more extreme forms of propaganda and the milder forms of underground activity is a slender one. Perhaps the best way of differentiating between the two is to say that propaganda is confined to activities which are generally considered to be within the law, whereas underground activities are outside the law, and if the participants are discovered they incur punishment and penalties. These definitions, which seem to be the best we can devise, are not, however, of uniform application and consequently not entirely satisfactory, because activities which are legal in one country may be illegal in another. The Democracies, and especially our own country, are particularly tolerant. In Britain and France to profess Communism is not a crime and, provided a Communist does not infringe the law applicable to all citizens, he is treated in the same manner as the members of other political parties. We have had Communist Members of Parliament enjoying the full rights and privileges of the House of Commons. In many countries of the Free World—such as South Africa—some restrictions are placed on known Communists, but these are mild when compared with the treatment of those who oppose Communism behind the Iron Curtain. There the rights of free thought, and the right to persuade others to one's way of thinking, are not tolerated. It is not only a crime to be anti-Communist but a crime not to be an active supporter of Communism.

In the previous chapter the importance of the "direct approach" form of propaganda was emphasized and this, in its application to our own country, is perhaps the best medium for demonstrating by example the difference between propaganda and underground activities. Any individual who is legally resident in this country, either permanently or temporarily, is at liberty to persuade others to his way of thought, so long as his actions are not treasonable, or otherwise contrary to law. He may make speeches, or statements, in public or in private; write articles, or letters, for the press; or even broadcast on the radio if he is given facilities to do so. That is propaganda and perfectly legal. If, however, his actions amount to treason, or he uses blackmail or any other illegal process, his activities become actionable, and he can only continue them, without incurring the penalties of the law, by underground means.

Underground activities may be described, therefore, as hostile activities which are contrary to the law of the country in which they are practised, and which, in consequence, have to be carried out in secret.

It is at once apparent that the term "Underground Activities" covers a very wide field, and one which is wider behind the Iron Curtain, where restrictions are severe, than in the more tolerant Democracies. In its mildest form it may mean some statement, or action, which just oversteps the border line of legal propaganda. In its most virulent form it may be incitement, or secret action, to carry out widespread sabotage, or even incitement or action to overthrow the government by force.

There are many methods of tabulating the activities which the term implies, but the following will suffice for our purpose:

(a) *Illegal propaganda*, i.e. propaganda carried out secretly which is treasonable or otherwise actionable. ("Subversive activities" is a suitable term.)

(b) "*Persuasion*" which is carried out by means of blackmail or threats, e.g. when a hostile agent, having discovered that an individual has done something illegal, threatens to expose him if he does not assist in furthering his aims.

(c) *Ordinary espionage*—the uncovering of secrets of a political, military or industrial nature.

(d) *Sabotage*—the destruction, or damaging, of military or civil installations or equipment, or the dislocation of military or civil organization.

(e) *Fermenting hostile military activities or open rebellion*, or the overthrow of government by the threat, or actual use, of force.

All these methods were employed extensively by both sides before and during the late war, and have been used since; and some amplification, and a few examples of how they operate, will not be out of place.

Prior to their occupation by the Germans in 1938–39 Austria and Czechoslovakia had both been "softened up" by a process which included subversive activities on a very extensive scale. The same technique was applied to Poland, but with different results, as the Poles decided to fight rather than submit, and thus the Second World War started. Much of the activity of Major Quisling in Norway,

UNDERGROUND ACTIVITIES

which culminated in the German invasion of Norway in April, 1940, consisted of subversive activities directed from Germany.

There are many degrees of "illegal persuasion" which have been employed with success. At its highest level it includes the methods of threat and intimidation to which President Hacha of Czechoslovakia was subjected in the spring of 1939, to induce him to sign an agreement for the German occupation of Prague, and making Bohemia and Moravia into a German Protectorate. At lower levels it is practised very frequently, and in a form which often results in the victim being almost unaware of the danger which assails him. The technique is to discover some minor irregularity, or to get the individual to commit himself in some trivial manner, but in a way which creates a dread of exposure. By a gradual intensification of "heat" an indiscreet, or gullible, individual is in time converted into a traitor or spy. This is the process by which many in the Democracies—students, Trade Union officials, industrialists, scientists, politicians and others have been won, unwillingly in many cases, to Communism. Their number must be legion. For every case which comes to light we can be sure there are very many which remain undisclosed.

Espionage has become almost an established and accepted custom; but it is not usually carried out in the dramatic manner of the more sensational novels. There are always a few professional international spies, but their information is mostly unreliable, they soon become recognized for what they are and they have a nasty habit of changing sides if it seems profitable to do so. No good secret service relies on these gentry; but rather on the part-time agent, who picks up what he can in the course of his legitimate trade, profession or occupation. One suspects that the organization and practice of espionage is a very dull and routine business, quite unlike the glamorous activities we read about in fiction. It is, however, always with us, and security measures in Government offices and establishments, in the Armed Forces and in Industry are a very important matter.

Sabotage may be of two kinds—material, such as arson to a ship or factory; or what may be termed moral sabotage, designed to disrupt organization, such as the fermenting of strikes, or the creation of hostility or apathy towards a project of national importance. The material kind is very difficult to recognize with certainty. When a ship catches fire in dock, a series of aircraft accidents occur, or an unexplained explosion occurs in an arms factory, one may suspect sabotage, and the suspicion is no doubt frequently justified, but there is rarely definite proof and the cause usually remains in doubt. With moral sabotage the position is different, as in many cases the origin is clear. Evidence is not lacking that very elaborate organizations exist in this country, in other Commonwealth countries and among our friends and allies, for the purpose of fermenting strikes, hindering recruiting for the regular armed forces, causing ill-discipline among servicemen and, by infiltration and other means, bringing public services, institutions and bodies into disrepute—The Church, Trade Unions, Industrial Organizations, Universities, Youth Movements, Local Councils, the Fire Service, Civil Defence Service and even the Civil Service. Perhaps the most dangerous of these activities is the unofficial strike, which in our own country and in some Commonwealth countries takes the form of strikes in defiance of the advice of responsible Trade Union leaders, and in France has resulted in refusals by dock workers to load military equipment and stores destined for Indo-China. There is ample evidence to show that this type of strike is inspired by Communists controlled from Moscow. Only recently it has been revealed that in many University cities and towns in this country the local Communist organization is at great pains to ensnare newly joined students—particularly Colonial students, by offering hospitality to men and women in a strange country. The word Communism is probably never mentioned. The victim becomes a "fellow traveller" and ultimately, in some cases, an avowed Communist, without realizing what is happening. Very often the methods are within the law and come under the heading of propaganda by direct approach; but this is not always so. In the process the dividing line between legal propaganda and illegal subversive activities is frequently crossed.

In our own country Communist efforts to ferment hostile military activities, or open rebellion, are not a very serious problem. The chances of success are remote, and it is doubtful if any serious attempts in this direction are likely. It is a matter which demands vigilance, but it is not a cause for alarm.

The pre-war, war and post-war years provide many examples of this kind of underground activity. Hitler was an adept at organizing armed Nazis in the countries he sought to annex—Austria, Czechoslovakia and Poland. These organizations began as underground movements, but usually came out into the open as the time for the coup drew near.

In all the occupied countries during the war years (1940–45) strong resistance movements—mostly organized and controlled from this

UNDERGROUND ACTIVITIES

country—were formed. By sabotage and other means these underground troops succeeded in pinning down large German forces which would otherwise have been used on the battle fronts. The Russian, Yugoslav, French, Norwegian, Polish and other partisans, and underground forces, played a great part in the defeat of Nazi Germany.*
Unfortunately in some countries, not Communist during the war, these partisans became affected by Communism. They and their successors, often under the same leadership, have been instrumental in bringing more than one country into the fold of the Iron Curtain, and there is evidence that in some countries of the Free World they still practise their underground activities—now on behalf of the Soviet.

As in most forms of underground activity the militant form embraces a variety of degrees. In its widest range it may provide succour and encouragement for rebels in Malaya, Indo-China or Kenya. It includes the provision of murder and kidnapping gangs in West Berlin and Western Germany and minor militant activities in many other countries.

The examples of underground activities given in this chapter merely provide a glimpse at the almost endless varieties of secret "warfare" which is going on all over the world. Unknown to the general public a bitter struggle is in progress between those who seek to wreck the existing order and replace it by their own ideology, and the counter-forces of law and order, which practically every country finds it necessary to maintain on a considerable scale.

It is difficult to get a true picture of the scope of, and degree of danger from, forces whose success depends on remaining undetected. There is, however, one aspect of this matter which requires the greatest emphasis and provides a fitting conclusion to this chapter. It can be stated in a few sentences:

There are two methods by which a country can become Communist, namely:

By Force or the Threat of Force

or

By the Ballot Box.

Of the two the Ballot Box is by far the more dangerous, although this was not perhaps the case 4 or 5 years ago.

* Those who desire more information on this subject should read *Secret Forces—The Technique of Underground Movements*, by F. O. Miksche (Faber and Faber, 15s.).

The intention to use force is usually well advertised in advance. It is nearly always contrary to the wishes of the majority of the people, and consequently any action to prevent it has the backing of legality. Now that the defences of the Free World are properly organized, and becoming stronger every day, it should be possible to frustrate any attempt to win a State to Communism by force from within, sponsored from without—as was done in Czechoslovakia in 1948.

The Ballot Box on the other hand has the blessing of legality, although we know how it can be abused in politically immature countries—those in which the economic and social conditions are bad and in which bribery and corruption play a part in public affairs.

Nevertheless, Democracy has taken its stand on Democratic representative government, and cannot deny to its opponents the rights which it claims for itself. There are many countries in the Free World with large minorities of Communists or "Fellow Travellers" and in which a Communist government, through the Ballot Box, is not inconceivable—France, Italy, India and others. If this happened it is difficult to see how we could do otherwise than accept the situation, provided the vote had been a free one and no illegal means had been employed. It is not difficult to appreciate, however, the adverse effect such an event might have on Democratic prestige, and on the defence of Western Europe and other vital interests.

Underground activity designed to promote Communism in the Free World, through the Ballot Box, is probably the most dangerous aspect of "The New Warfare".

CHAPTER VI

LIMITED "HOT WAR" AND WAR BY PROXY

IF you think it will be profitable to engage in war; but realize you cannot afford the cost, and risks, of a major conflict, the next best thing is to arrange a small, or limited, war. If you can get somebody else to do the fighting, without yourself forfeiting the advantages, it would seem that you are "on velvet", as they say in racing circles.

This is what Russia has succeeded in doing in Indo-China and in Korea, and to a less extent in Malaya.

It so happens that the present Eastern theatres of war are examples of limited war and (from the Soviet point of view) war by proxy as well. This may not always be the case, however, and as we are considering long-term events it will be best to examine "limited" and "proxy" war separately.

Limited War

Limited war may be defined as war in which the resources of one (or both) of the belligerents are not extended to the full. This is no new thing: it is as old as war itself, and in fact the British have been one of its chief exponents. By means of sea power we have often, as Bacon said, been able to take as much, or as little, of the war as we desired. Prior to 1914 many of our wars were limited wars. The conquest of India, the Crimean War and the South African War, although not inconsiderable, did not tax us to the full, and all our innumerable Colonial wars were limited wars.

In the past it was a simple matter to control a limited war. They were usually fought against enemies who were not highly organized, and not bound by alliances likely to lead to the conflict spreading. The issue was rarely in doubt, although hostilities often became unduly prolonged owing to an under-estimation of the enemy, and our proverbial policy of sending a boy on a man's job.

Nevertheless, there are instances of wars, which were started on a limited basis, getting out of hand and eventually far exceeding in scope and duration the intentions of those who started them. The Peninsular War (1808–14) and the South African War (1899–1902) are examples. Both were started as small enterprises, with a few thousand troops, and grew in size far beyond the original conceptions. There are, of course, many instances of campaigns (as opposed to wars) starting in a modest way and ending by absorbing resources far in excess of the original intentions. The Gallipoli campaign of 1915, started as a Naval enterprise, eventually involved British and French land forces amounting to several divisions. When the Italians invaded Egypt in 1940 they anticipated an easy victory against the weak Commonwealth forces opposing them. The campaign ultimately involved the destruction of the cream of the Italian Army and later proved a heavy drain on German resources.

It can be said, however, that up to comparatively recent times wars could be kept under control. A conflict might assume somewhat larger proportions than was anticipated; but it was unlikely that one started as a small incident would become a world-wide struggle. This is not the case to-day. Nations are organized in large groups, each member of which is bound by treaty, or alliance, to assist any other member who is in trouble. Travel by sea and land has been speeded up and a new element, the air, has been introduced which makes the movement of personnel, stores and equipment an immensely faster process than was the case 50 years ago. Consequently the practical difficulties of assembling, and maintaining, large forces have been reduced.

As a result the great powers take pains to cloak any warlike incident which they may start, or sponsor, in a guise which they hope will confine it to the limits which suit their purpose. Modern history is full of examples demonstrating that this is no easy matter and that miscalculations are very apt to occur. Herr Hitler, when he invaded Poland in 1939, hoped that the powers would stand aside, as they had done in the cases of Austria and Czechoslovakia. He hardly expected to provoke a world war of nearly six years' duration, which would end with his own death and the ruin of Nazi Germany. When, in the summer of 1950, the United Nations under the initial lead of America, decided to support the South Koreans against the North Koreans the extent of the conflict was obviously not foreseen. Similarly the French in Indo-China could not have anticipated the immense drain of this campaign in men, money and material.

Nevertheless, it can be said that Korea and Indo-China in the 1950s have not led to disaster on the scale that Poland did in 1939. Why is this, and how is it that we have been able to check the play of forces in a manner which we failed to do in 1939? There are several reasons; but undoubtedly the most important is that neither group of powers can afford a large-scale shooting war: they will do almost anything to prevent one.* Subsidiary reasons are that the theatres of war are remote from the home lands of the leading powers, and that the areas in dispute are not *vital* to any great power. Korea is of little economic importance to anybody, except the Koreans. Indo-China, whilst of considerable importance economically, is not *vital* to the existence of France.

It is, however, obvious that the continuance of these limited wars —in which great powers are either directly involved, or acting as sponsors—is a very real danger to world peace. In both theatres— more pronounced perhaps in Korea than in Indo-China—we have the remarkable spectacle of one side being provisioned from, and having its line of supply in, what is nominally a neutral country; but which is actually a "preserved" zone which the other side shrinks to assault for fear of enlarging the area of conflict, and perhaps starting a Third World War of the shooting kind. It is a measure of the extent to which the Free World is prepared to go that America summarily dismissed from the Supreme Command the man who was her leading general, a national hero, and who had shown marked ability in the conduct of operations—merely because he advocated measures which, although militarily correct, might have caused an extension of the war. We are prepared to accept conditions which make it almost impossible to win, rather than provoke a large-scale shooting war. It would seem that the Soviet is of the same mind, judging by the meticulous manner in which she confines her part to advice and encouragement, and avoids active participation in the fighting. We must not, however, be deceived by this. It is still possible—there are some who think probable—that the Soviet means war in Europe. If this is so, existing conditions in Korea and Indo-China could hardly suit her purpose better. Hundreds of thousands of American and European troops are engaged there, to the detriment of N.A.T.O. defence in Europe, and not a single Russian soldier is similarly diverted. This is a strategic conception which the great masters of war of the past would have hardly conceived to be possible. The renewed hopes of a cease fire in Korea have not resulted in any slackening of Communist activities elsewhere in the Far East.

* Prior to February, 1953, when President Eisenhower modified the order, the 7th U.S.A. Fleet had the assignment of preventing hostilities between Communist China and Chinese Nationalist Forces in Formosa. This is contrary to hitherto accepted standards for the conduct of war and shows the lengths to which the Free World is prepared to go to prevent an extension of the Korean War. Reluctance to institute a blockade of Communist China is another example, although other considerations also play a part in this attitude.

War by Proxy

The more we examine in detail the methods of "The New Warfare" the more we come to realize that there is little connected with it which is new in conception—only in the scope and integration of the methods.

War by proxy is a very ancient institution: indeed the cynic might well say that there must be something wrong with a man who fights his own battles in preference to getting a reliable substitute to fight them for him. The British have practised the system on many occasions, although more in the sense of employing mercenaries as allies, or partners, rather than as the sole participants in a war in British interests. We have never quite succeeded in persuading a country to fight our battles single-handed, without our participation, and against its own interests—as it would seem Russia has persuaded the Chinese to do in Korea.

The war in Korea demonstrates the remarkable hold which Communism has on its adherents. It is apparent that even a complete Communist victory would give China little advantage to compensate for the very considerable sacrifices she is making. It is indeed surprising that the Pekin Government ever agreed to participate on such a large scale. Having done so, one would have expected the troops engaged to do so with little enthusiasm for a cause which they can hardly understand, and which affects them only indirectly. The Chinese are not a warlike race, and prior to the advent of Communism showed little skill at military organization, and little prowess as fighters. Nevertheless, all reports indicate that the Chinese armies in Korea are well organized, well led, adequately equipped and are fighting with skill and, frequently, with fanatical courage. This is the more remarkable in view of the marked air superiority of the United Nations, which has resulted in very heavy, and continuous, bombing attacks on the Chinese rear areas—a condition which usually results in a deterioration in morale; but which has not done so in this case.

The fact that Soviet encouragement and assistance can produce these startling results is a matter for deep thought, and concern, in the Free World. If similar results could be achieved elsewhere, there seems to be no limit to the extent to which the Communist cause might be furthered by the Russian policy of way by proxy.

It would seem that the answer lies in making proxy warfare, not only unprofitable, but costly and unpleasant, for those who do the fighting. No doubt it was right to discard the policy recommended by General MacArthur, which would have inevitably extended the war to dangerous limits; but the fact remains that since he vacated command operations have degenerated into a state of unenterprising siege warfare. With their superior equipment, and command of the sea and air, it should have been possible for the United Nations' forces to undertake bold amphibious operations, including airborne operations, within the confines of Korea, with the object of winning a resounding victory. By such methods the Chinese might well have been disheartened, it might have produced a serious cleavage between China and the senior Axis partner and discouraged others contemplating the role of proxy fighters. It is not contended that these desirable results would have been certain; but there would have been a good chance of success; whereas the policy adopted for the past 2 years is probably exactly what our opponents want. It may be that in view of the interminable, and abortive, peace talks which took place earlier it was thought undesirable to make the war too hot; but if this is the reason, it is clear that Eastern methods of negotiating have been seriously misjudged. It was surely apparent to the meanest intellect that these negotiations would last just as long as it suited Soviet policy for them to continue.

There are two lessons to be learnt from Korea, namely:

(*a*) Provided you have an option in the matter, it is a mistake to embark on a "Hot-War" campaign unless there is a good chance of winning, and winning quickly.

(*b*) If you *are* engaged in a "Hot War" there is only one method of fighting—"all out" with every available means. In the case of Korea the political consideration of not extending the war area had to be taken into account; but a much greater effort, in Korea itself, should have been possible. Some remarks attributed to General Van Fleet, on his retirement from command in Korea, indicate that he, too, is of that opinion, and that failure to fight more aggressively within the Peninsula itself was due to considerations other than military.

It is surprising that some military commentators have stated that the Korean campaign is being waged without either side having an aim or object. Attention to the old, and simple, military principles should correct this belief.

For the United Nations the course is clear—to kill, or capture, every Communist fighting man in Korea, and to apply the same treatment to any reinforcements which venture South of the Yalu

River. There is at least a chance that even a partial success in this direction would make the war unpopular in Pekin.

The Communist object is perhaps more obscure. If the aim is to occupy the whole of Korea, which is probably the one China favours, then the object is to drive the United Nations forces into the sea. If, on the other hand, it is to contain as many United Nations troops as possible in a remote part of Asia, which would seem to be to the Soviet's advantage, it is clear that the present stalemate situation is entirely satisfactory.

There is every indication that limited war and war by proxy, or the threat of war by proxy, are likely to play an increasing part in Soviet plans. In this connection it is interesting to note the approximate strengths of some potential proxy forces:

	Treaty Limit	Actual Strength (Feb. 1953)
East Germany	Reliable reports indicate that an army of about 500,000 East Germans, organized into three corps, exists.	
Hungary	70,000	175,000
Rumania	138,000	250,000
Bulgaria	65,000	175,000

CHAPTER VII

THE ARMED ARRAY

It has been emphasized in earlier chapters that "The New Warfare" is the modern substitute for the full-scale shooting wars of 1914–18 and 1939–45. Nevertheless, both groups of powers are maintaining large forces by sea, land and air, in a condition which would enable them to be brought into action instantly in a Third World War, fought with atomic weapons. In Western Europe these forces are facing each other in close proximity, not altogether unlike the conditions in the winter of 1939–40 when, during the "phoney war", French and German troops faced each other from their fortified lines on either side of the Franco-German frontier. The patrol activities in 1939–40 were in some ways similar to the clashes between East and West police and military which now occur in Berlin. Behind the array of conventional forces we may be sure that atomic-bomb carrying aircraft, and other nuclear weapons, are in instant readiness.

These immense armaments are a crushing burden to both sides, and the main cause of economic instability, and delays in post-war rehabilitation, throughout the world. As "The New Warfare" does not visualize large-scale fighting—but only limited and proxy warfare—one may well inquire the reason for these large forces, which may never be used.

There are two reasons:

For bargaining purposes or, to put it more bluntly, for the purpose of threatening

It has long been a principle of international diplomacy that argument is mostly useless unless backed by force—a principle which we have often failed, and our opponents frequently been at pains, to observe.

As insurance policies

The main reason for the substitution of "New Warfare" for "Shooting Warfare" methods is mutual fear of the cost and destruction, and the uncertainty of the outcome. Clearly these conditions would not exist if one group were overwhelmingly more powerful than the other. The weaker would have no option but to accede to the other's demands, however unreasonable.

The rival groups resemble the two Victorian families living side by side, who vied with each other in the manner of dressing, and entertaining for, their numerous daughters. To maintain, by this means, the prestige of their respective families became the main occupation of both pairs of parents, and in the end they both went bankrupt in the process.

If for any reason the Armed Array ceases to fulfil its "insurance" role it could only mean that "New Warfare" methods had ended and a shooting war had started. For the purpose of this study it will, therefore, only be necessary to consider the bargaining, or threatening, role.*

Again, there is nothing new in this. No nation, however powerful or confident of victory, goes to war if it can gain its ends by other means. The other means is diplomacy, which throughout the ages has, almost invariably, depended for success on the adequacy of its backing by force. On occasions the comparative skill of the rival diplomats has been a factor and sometimes the ethics of the case, or the generosity of one side; but, in the main, the threat of force has been the chief consideration in international affairs.

From this emerged a variety of conditions which have governed, and to some extent still govern, international relations. Of these the two most important were:

Firstly. Nations became allied in opposing groups in the hope of obtaining approximate equality. This policy—a traditional one for the British in Europe—was designed to protect the weak, and by creating uncertainty as to the result, reduce the chances of war. It was frequently successful in preventing war, but when war *did* occur it was on a much larger scale. It might well be argued that the balance of power was the cause of the First World War, as the various alliances turned a minor incident into a Continental, and eventually a world-wide, issue.

Secondly. In areas where the balance of power did not, or could not, operate, small nations tended to come under the protection of one or more powerful ones. The best example is the relation-

---

* The "proxy" value of East German and Soviet Satellite State forces is indicated on page 38.

ship between the U.S.A. and the South American countries. Others are our own relations, from time to time, with Egypt, Persia and Iraq.

As the First World War showed that the balance of power was unreliable as a means of preventing war the Powers, on the conclusion of hostilities in 1918, sought other means of preserving peace. The result was "The League of Nations", which was instituted with the main object of substituting arbitration for war, and which hoped, should the necessity arise, to enforce its decisions by economic pressure (or sanctions) and, as a last resort, by combined force against the recalcitrant country or countries. From the outset the League was at a disadvantage in not including the U.S.A. Although it performed good work in the social and economic spheres it proved useless for preserving peace. Japanese aggression in China, Italian aggression in Abyssinia, the German occupations of Austria and Czechoslovakia, and finally the Second World War—all showed the impotence of the League.

The second recent attempt to preserve peace by this means produced the United Nations Organization, which although it includes the U.S.A., and is in many ways an improvement on the League, falls lamentably short of expectations. Indeed, it is difficult to imagine what further steps the nations could have taken to jeopardize the success of U.N.O., other than those they have actually taken. Matters of the gravest concern to the whole world are considered not on their merits, but on a strictly party, or group, line. The same nations vote together, and in the same manner, every time; their only criterion being that they vote against their customary opponents. Reasonable proposals for compromise and understanding—such as India's Korean peace proposals—are turned down so swiftly, and emphatically, that it is clear that they have not been even considered. In the Security Council the machinery of the veto is abused in a manner never contemplated by its designers, and hardly comprehensible in an assembly charged with the solemn duty of maintaining peace for all mankind.

U.N.O. may have served a useful purpose by keeping contact between the representatives of West and East; but it suffers from the disabilities inherent in any organization of its kind, which is not founded on goodwill and a genuine desire by all to achieve the purpose for which it was brought into existence.

A cursory survey of the problem shows that the existing array of armed might—based on conscription, a state of semi-mobilization and arms production on a scale akin to the war years—is no passing phase; but one which we may have to endure for many decades. There are a variety of reasons for this, which may be summarized as follows:

(*a*) The uncompromising attitude of the two world groups, which gives both the impression that all would be lost if they did not safeguard their interests by maintaining strong forces to deter their opponents.

(*b*) The apparent equality of the two groups—the Soviet having superiority in man-power: the West in equipment and scientific methods. This gives both the feeling that their chances of victory in another shooting war hang on a slender thread, and that, unless they employ the maximum number of men and amount of material, they may suffer defeat. Thus we have large conscript Sea, Land and Air Forces, lavishly provided with weapons, and other equipment which requires replacement every few years—all on a scale which world economy can only just support.

(*c*) There are also certain economic and social aspects of the matter which, from a short-term angle, make conscription, and arms production, a welcome condition. In the Soviet, and perhaps even more so in the Satellite countries, the young manhood of the country is much more easily controlled under military discipline, and in organized arms factories, than in normal civil life—even a regimented civil life. The withdrawal of those in the armed forces from peaceful pursuits is not very serious in a country which is still in process of developing its industry, where luxury production is not demanded and where forced labour is an established institution. In the Free West, in times of real peace, unemployment has always been an important factor in the price Democracy has to pay for its liberties. It is true to say that unemployment, and the shadow of unemployment, is our greatest social evil. In this country we have escaped; but other countries—including the great and prosperous United States of America—have suffered mass unemployment. Conscription helps to mitigate this condition; and if, by some miracle, a sudden large reduction in military establishments was brought about, there might be very serious

THE ARMED ARRAY

temporary unemployment. In some countries, badly disorganized by the war, conscription is not unwelcome as a stabilizing influence, and a backing to the civil police, for the preservation of law and order.

Although this great array of might everywhere is maintained chiefly for military purposes, it will be seen that there are also economic, social and political sides to the matter.

The aspects which concern us most are the manner in which these forces can be used in "The New Warfare" (as distinct from their employment in a full-scale shooting war) and the extent to which they are likely to promote another total war. It must be admitted that our experience of present-day conditions is very limited. Prior to the Napoleonic Wars large forces did not threaten peace, because they were rarely maintained. Compared to modern experiences the forces employed were trivial, and the tendency was for armies to be raised for a particular war; not to maintain them, as we do now, in case there might be a war. In this country we usually—not always—maintained a strong and efficient fleet; but it was our invariable practice, right up to 1939, to raise an army after the declaration of war, or when hostilities were imminent.

On the Continent this system changed with Napoleon, who showed the way to the nation in arms and started the fashion for maintaining large conscript armies. It was not, however, until the war of 1914-18 that the system of the nation in arms was perfected. It was not until 1945 that the world fully realized that total war was almost equally disastrous for the victors as for the vanquished; that 10 years of slaughter and destruction in a period of just over 30 years had brought us all to the verge of disaster, and that another full-scale war—with the "improved" atomic weapons—would almost certainly wipe out all traces of existing civilization. Moreover, it was apparent to all that if mankind could only give up war, and preparations for war, the prospect of a golden age, with necessities and luxuries for everybody, was not a figment of the imagination, but a practical possibility.*

---

* There are, of course, some who dispute the possibilities of ever realizing these conditions. They maintain that war is man's inheritance, and natural element, and that without it he would in time degenerate physically, morally and socially. As mankind as a whole has never been at peace for any considerable period it is difficult to judge the validity of this argument. It is, however, borne out, to some extent, by the rapid deterioration of some primitive races and tribes when deterred from war by European colonization. It may well be that athletics, and sport, are the true substitute for war.

Although it may be true that in the past the maintenance of large forces—or what were then considered to be large forces—brought about war, it is not necessarily true to-day. Prior to 1914 the consequences of war were disastrous for a few, very inconvenient for many, but of little matter to the majority. Some even gained solid advantages. The years 1914–18 only partially convinced the world that 20th-century total war far exceeded all previous experiences in its evil effect. It took the Second World War to confirm this view, and now that both West and East are capable of employing atomic weapons on a scale which increases from day to day, the importance of avoiding a Third World War is hardly in dispute among intelligent people.

The conditions of to-day are clearly quite different from any which existed previously. The decisions to go to war made by Napoleon, Bismarck, Kaiser William II and Hitler can be regarded as almost trivial compared to a decision to start a full-scale world war in the Atomic Age.

We need not, therefore, be too pessimistic because armed strength has previously resulted in war: it is by no means inevitable that it will bring about a full-scale shooting war again. The stakes are altogether different and every responsible person knows they are different.

It is, however, evident that so long as the means exist on a great scale there must continue to be some danger. The decision might rest with a few men—possibly only one man—and history gives no cause for confidence in the wisdom of Dictators in matters of this kind. The best we can say is that the position is not hopeless. As a deterrent there is the example of those who in 1914 and in 1939 made war, with the odds apparently greatly in their favour, but who brought disaster to themselves and ruin to their country.

There is also always the chance that war may result by some miscalculation of the effect of a threat or demand, or misjudgment of the fibre of an opponent. A hand may be overplayed and a threat exceed the limit of the other side's willingness to compromise. "Appeasement" is a word which we have grown to dislike. Both World Wars started with miscalculations of this kind. Up to the very last the Germans in 1914 believed that we would not honour our guarantee to Belgium and that there was a good chance of our standing aside. In 1939 Hitler had been assured by Ribbentrop that Britain would not fight under any circumstances, and our previous conduct in the Czechoslovakian crisis seemed to confirm this belief.

THE ARMED ARRAY

He entered on his Polish adventure under the impression that it was at least a good risk that France and Britain would not intervene.

This is perhaps a suitable place to mention a characteristic of modern war equipment which appears to have escaped public notice, but which merits closer examination. In 1944 the Germans bombarded London and the South of England with pilotless aircraft (V1) and rockets (V2). These missiles had a much longer range than any hitherto used in war. Since then, long range weapons of the rocket type have been greatly improved. Ranges of several hundred miles have been attained, and so great is the speed of modern scientific development that it is no flight of the imagination to say that ranges of thousands of miles may be attained in a very short time. If such missiles carried an atomic charge it does not require a great deal of imagination to appreciate their potentialities. This is, however, only one aspect of the matter.

It will also be clear that with weapons having these long ranges it might be very difficult to identify the user, or establish the locality from which they were fired, as was the case with the German V1s and V2s in 1944. For purposes of argument we will assume that large detonations (atomic or otherwise) occurred in the neighbourhood of Paris or London, under circumstances that indicated that the missiles had been fired from a long-range projector of the rocket type. It would be possible for all to disclaim responsibility, or knowledge, of the incidents. An accusation directed to the most obvious quarter might bring the reply, "We know nothing about it: possibly if you inquired in Berne, Madrid or Reykjavík you would get some information." It may be that precision instruments, or some other means of locating the area of origin of such missiles, exist; but it seems unlikely that they would be efficient under all conditions.

This possibility exposes two very real dangers, namely:

(*a*) That concentrations of missiles of this kind might be used to obtain a "flying start" in a Third World War. Retaliation, by similar or other means, might be seriously delayed, because the country responsible could not be established with certainty.

or

(*b*) These methods might be employed by proxy—the missiles being fired by, and from, a Satellite State, the senior partner disclaiming all knowledge of the matter. This is a form of "The New Warfare" against which we should be on our guard.

The spectacle of the Armed Array is a grim one, which can be summarized in a few sentences:

While it exists there is always the danger of another total war, brought about by accident or design.

We need not, however, assume that, because in the past the building up of large forces has always been followed by war, another shooting war on a world scale is inevitable. It could have occurred at any time within the past 7 years; but it has not occurred.

The continuance of power politics by means of threats is certain, and the employment of new, and novel, means of getting some dividend from the immense forces being maintained is to be expected.

There is little chance of an early agreement between East and West for mutual disarmament on a worth-while scale. The process of disarmament will be a very long-term one, and if we value our security and freedom we must become reconciled to the burden of heavy armaments, and national service, for many years.

CHAPTER VIII

OBSTRUCTION AND PLANNED INCONVENIENCES

THIS penultimate chapter, which may be termed the "residue" chapter, deals with certain activities in "The New Warfare" which have not been discussed previously, as they do not fall conveniently under earlier headings and definitions.

A superficial investigation of the annoyances practised by the Soviet and her friends against the Free World gives the impression that they are perpetrated solely to irritate, as a man might turn on the wireless at full blast, or light a bonfire in his garden, merely to annoy a neighbour. Careful study, however, indicates that this is not so, and that the inconveniences to which we are continuously subjected are mostly carefully designed for a definite purpose—to cause friction between Allies, to divert resources from one place to another, to gain time or for some other purpose not always easy to recognize.

These activities take many forms. Often they are at a high level, sometimes obviously directed from Moscow: in others they are clearly initiated locally. In certain cases they are by proxy, the main Communist partner not being directly involved. Always they conform to a policy whose origin is unmistakable.

All these abuses have, however, a factor in common with other activities in "The New Warfare": although frequently unreasonable in the extreme they almost invariably have a façade of legality and they are not pursued to lengths likely to involve the Soviet Union in a shooting war. This confirms the view that our opponents have no desire to provoke a Third World War; but whether this is merely a temporary attitude, because the time is not yet judged to be opportune, or a permanent policy, is debatable.

In the past few years the number of incidents in this category has been very large. On a major scale they are considerable, and minor activities are of daily occurrence in the areas where Communist and Democratic forces, or nationals, abut. It would be impossible to tabulate a comprehensive list, but a few examples, with some comments, will be helpful.

THE NEW WARFARE

Communications with West Berlin

West Berlin is an "island" surrounded by Soviet-controlled territory; but by agreement America, Britain and France have certain rights of way by road, rail, water and air into the city. Efforts to interrupt the land communications have been almost continuous—sometimes comparatively mild, sometimes intense and exasperating. In the air the slightest deviation, or alleged deviation, from the agreed "corridor" in and out of West Berlin has led to menacing threats by Soviet fighter aircraft, if not actual attack. The interruption of land communications usually takes the form of imposing some new regulation, such as a new kind of pass for personnel or a new method of packing or inspecting stores. These measures are said to be necessary safety precautions or for the purpose of checking espionage. It is by these means that the Russians contrive to give an air of legality to their actions. In most cases there is no actual legal justification; but even if there were, this is indeed strange behaviour by a country against its nominal Allies and fellow members of U.N.O., while engaged in occupying the territory of a defeated common enemy. Moreover, by any standards of reasonableness, there is no excuse for this attitude, as the other occupying powers have been meticulous in their relations with the Soviet authorities.

The peak of friction was reached in 1948, when all land communications between the West and West Berlin were cut, and America, Britain and France organized the famous "Berlin Air-lift", by means of which troops and civilians were maintained with essentials by air. This operation appears to have surprised our opponents by its scale, efficiency and effectiveness; but not for months was the land blockade lifted, by which time the air operations had cost millions of pounds and the troops and German civilians in West Berlin suffered great inconvenience and, in some cases, considerable hardship. Since then, interruptions in communications have continued, but on a comparatively minor scale.

The circumstances which necessitated the "Berlin Air-lift" are an outstanding example of obstruction and planned inconveniences in the most acute form—clearly carried out with the intention of ejecting the Western powers from Berlin.

The Use of the Veto in the Security Council of U.N.O.

This is not the place to explain the origin of the veto, or the wisdom of having such a curious rule; but when U.N.O. was established it was not unreasonable to suppose that, after 6 years of total war, all nations would show a sense of responsibility, and make a genuine effort to further the chief aim of the organization—peace and goodwill everywhere.

The Soviet has abused this rule, and it is difficult to find a reason, other than a planned attempt to use U.N.O. to further World Communism.

The Korean Peace Talks

The peace talks between the United Nations representatives on the one hand and those of China and North Korea on the other, which have been going on for so long,* are one of the most fatuous exhibitions seen in international relations. It is true that they were initiated in somewhat unusual circumstances. Armistice terms are more normally discussed when one nation, or group, has gained a decisive victory. In such conditions Marshal Foch in 1918, Herr Hitler with France in 1940 and General Eisenhower in 1945 were able to impose terms within a few hours. In Korea things were quite different, as operations were in a condition of stalemate; but with all the negotiating advantages on the side of the Communists. We must assume that Korean war policy is controlled from Moscow, and it was, at the time, obviously to the Soviet's advantage that this proxy campaign should continue indefinitely. As soon as one bone of contention was resolved the Communists raised another, and so it went on, and may still go on, for as long as the Kremlin regards war in Korea as profitable.

The nuisance tactics at the Korean Peace Talks are an example of the cruder methods of obstruction employed by our opponents.

Russian Wives of British Subjects

Russia has persistently refused to permit the Russian wives of a few British service and ex-service men to leave Russia to join their husbands. Although the numbers involved are small, and the matter hardly one of major importance, it has been the subject of diplomatic representation at the highest level. The late Mr. Ernest Bevin, when he was Foreign Secretary, approached the Soviet on more than one occasion and their refusal then, and since, was clearly a high-level decision. To have conceded this point would have cost the Russians nothing, and no possible loss of face, or prestige, would have

---

* At the time of writing (May, 1953) the talks have recently been reopened after having been discontinued for a considerable time.

followed. If there had existed the slightest desire to make a gesture of goodwill, this matter provided a good opportunity; but it was not accepted.

The above are examples of high-level obstruction. The following are a few typical examples on a lower, or local, level.

Restrictions on travel and movement

It is not easy to obtain admission to Russia, or Soviet-controlled countries. Having got permission it is harder still to enjoy a free and unfettered view of conditions, as would be normal in our own and other Democratic countries. Although, for obvious reasons, those visiting Russia for a short period for some "peace" conference, or other purpose, are usually treated with hospitality; our Embassy staffs, and others with official assignments, are subjected to severe restrictions and live under the shadow of a constant, and undisguised, system of surveillance. By irksome methods life is made difficult for them.

This is partly in accord with the general policy of obstruction and planned inconveniences; but may be in part due to reluctance to allow Westerners to see some of the more sordid conditions behind the Iron Curtain. Similarly, the aloofness of Russian diplomats, and other officials assigned to the Free World, is probably due to a policy designed to prevent close contact with people whose standard of living is so immeasurably higher than that enjoyed by the majority in the Soviet.

Minor incidents against individuals, vehicles, aircraft, etc.

All over the world, but particularly in Europe, other minor incidents occur almost daily, as part of the deliberate policy to hinder any improvement in relations between East and West.

A British or American soldier, or a vehicle from West Berlin, by mistake enters East Berlin, perhaps trespassing only a few yards within Soviet-controlled territory, but is at once detained. Irksome inquiries follow, and it may be some days before the personnel, or vehicle, are returned, and then only as a result of tedious negotiations obviously designed to annoy.

An Allied aircraft may, through some misfortune, be forced to land in Soviet, or Satellite, territory. The help and sympathy expected for airmen in trouble is rarely extended. The crews are treated like enemy personnel in war, and requests for permission to salve the aircraft are frequently ignored or frustrated. Similarly a Western

OBSTRUCTION AND PLANNED INCONVENIENCES

aircraft flying over Eastern territory by mistake is treated as a hostile plane on a warlike mission. There have been cases of refusal to cooperate in search and rescue work in aircraft mishaps in waters which the Soviet claims to control.

It is difficult to fathom the reasons for this pin-prick policy of small-scale hindrance and annoyance. It is no doubt part of the policy of segregating the East from the West as far as possible. It is also probably due to a desire of subordinates to ingratiate themselves with their superiors, by adopting a "tough" attitude—or indeed fear of the consequences if they were friendly or cooperative.

The foregoing examples are typical of many similar incidents in this somewhat baffling aspect of West and East relations. In the more important activities in this category it is usually possible to find a reason—such as the time-wasting value of the Korean peace talks; but in the minor annoyances, initiated by local subordinates, the answer is not always clear. As suggested earlier it may be due to policy instructions issued from above, or to fear of not appearing "tough", or it may be that Communism inspires among its adherents such hatred for their opponents that they cannot bring themselves to adopt even a measure of cold civility. It would seem that the last is an unlikely reason and that the true one is a combination of the other two—deliberate policy and natural fear.

It will be noted in the course of reading this book that most activities of "The New Warfare" are not new, but merely adaptations of old policies, and methods, to modern conditions. The system of obstruction and planned inconveniences which we see to-day is somewhat different. In the past diplomacy was usually conducted under a veneer of politeness and good manners. Countries might be bitterly hostile, even on the verge of war, but a sense of decorum was usual. Even in war some seemliness was often observed.

The present trend is, therefore, somewhat of a novelty, and incidents occur, and are forgotten by the time another one occurs within a week or so, which, under the more formal diplomacy of the 1890s, would have been taken very seriously. The reason for this appears to be a fundamental one—we are at a stage in world affairs not previously experienced, with all human races grouped in a manner which extenuates their differences in ideology, outlook and behaviour to a marked degree. When the war ended the West, whilst not agreeing with the Soviet system or methods, was prepared to extend the hand of friendship, and to accord to Russia pride of place in the defeat of Germany, and the consequent high place in their regard which this implied. This was not accepted, and very soon Russia became obsessed with the belief that her late Allies were attempting to encircle her. It is indeed a tragedy that since 1945 hostility has become so acute, and behaviour degenerated to incidents of the kind described in this chapter.

It is, of course, wrong to imagine that these tactics are confined entirely to the Soviet and her friends. It would be hardly reasonable to expect the Democracies to forgo any reprisals. Indeed one of the most lamentable results of Soviet tactics on this count is the reciprocal suspicion which it has produced in the Democratic world. Any peace offers, or other high-level suggestions from the Communist side, tend to be treated with scepticism. Among individuals, on the comparatively rare occasions when they meet under tranquil conditions, a similar state of suspicion exists.

It is a prerequisite to any improvement in general relationship that this policy of annoyance and bad manners should stop. Although not insignificant they are, in themselves, perhaps the least serious aspect of "The New Warfare"; but they create a bad atmosphere everywhere and aggravate difficulties in other spheres. A little politeness and goodwill, even kindness, in these small matters would go far to creating conditions favourable for peaceful co-existence, which is discussed in the next chapter, and which is perhaps the best solution we can expect to our grievous problems.

CHAPTER IX

HOW WILL IT END?

The Trend of World Events, and some Suggestions for Future Policy

It is a great mistake, but a very common one, to suppose that peace is the normal condition of mankind. This is not so: *homo sapiens* is among the most pugnacious of living creatures and, judging by the results achieved in the past 40 years, modern man is even more ferocious than his predecessors. The history of the world is mostly the story of man fighting man, in groups of ever-increasing size and with weapons which produce greater and greater slaughter and destruction.

The idea that there could be universal, and permanent, peace is something quite new, and a theory which would have been considered ridiculous by most people prior to the 20th century. Our Divorce Courts, and an examination of family life, show that it is no easy matter to get two people, who have voluntarily selected each other as life partners, to agree. A study of our Parliamentary and Local Government procedure makes apparent how difficult it is to get a body of people, speaking the same language, and with a common interest, to see eye to eye. Is it really reasonable to expect an assembly like U.N.O. to agree—representing, as it does, more than fifty nations; with opposing, rather than common, interests; speaking many languages and composed of delegates of widely different colours, creeds, origin and outlook? The answer is at once clear—it would be remarkable, and contrary to all previous experience, if U.N.O. attained any considerable measure of agreement on any subject of importance. We must, therefore, accept the fact that continued discord between the nations is much more likely than the universal peace which so many expect, but which has so far baffled our efforts. On the other hand, although it would be foolish to expect perfection in human relations we must not accept tension at the present high tempo as permanent; indeed there are signs that some easement is probable—not perhaps in the immediate future, but as a long-term possibility.

A study of the evolution of mankind provides a ray of hope. In primitive times small-scale war between tribes and clans went on unceasingly. In a small area, perhaps no larger than an English county, several feuds, or skirmishes, might be in progress at the same time. As communities became organized into larger groups—such as our own Kingdoms of Wessex, Mercia, etc.—war became less frequent, but on a more formal, and larger, scale when it *did* occur. Later, small States and nations tended to combine to form larger units (e.g. Great Britain, Germany, the U.S.A.) and by the end of the 19th century the tendency of nations to organize in groups, for defensive purposes, became manifest. By 1914 this grouping had become so pronounced, and complicated, that a war involving any of the great powers was almost certain to involve others and become a world war.

From this we are able to deduce that during the process of evolution man has retained his warlike habits; but that as he became highly organized wars declined in frequency, but, when they *did* occur, increased very greatly in scope and severity. We appear to have run full cycle and in 1953 have reached the stage when the world consists of only two groups—Western Democracy and Eastern Communism. What is the next step to be—the final stage in man's evolution in relation to war? The two groups can either fight it out, in which case they will very likely—some think almost certainly—destroy all semblance of civilization everywhere; or they can settle their differences by peaceful means.

Another very important factor—a moral one, in contrast to the material one just discussed—is man's tendency throughout the ages to become obsessed with the belief that other men are plotting for his downfall, or are bitterly hostile to everything he does. The religious hatreds of the Middle Ages—between Christians and Infidels and, within the Christian communities, between Catholics and Protestants—are good examples. The suspicions of Americans for Britain in the 1890's and Hitler and his Nazis' intense hatred of the Jews, and all their works, are more modern examples.

Although obsessions of this kind still persist in many parts of the world, they are becoming less common. Men and women of different religions now find it possible to live in the same street and even in the same house. Our universities contain students of varying colours and races and, although they may not become intimate friends, they live and work side by side amicably. In many countries Trade Unionists and Capitalists bargain and argue in small matters,

HOW WILL IT END?

but can often be persuaded to agree if the issue is sufficiently serious.

We have gone a long way to abolish, or assuage, bitterness and hostility due to religion, colour, race, occupation and class; but in place of what were comparatively minor causes of friction we now find a new one, which divides the whole world, and divides it with a bitterness and degree of hatred exceeding anything known in the Dark Ages.

For all practical purposes there is only one bone of contention to-day—the difference of ideology of Democracy and Communism.

It is the purpose of this final chapter to suggest, or point the way to, a solution of this problem—the problem which affects all mankind so acutely, and looks as if it may persist for many decades. In seeking a solution a high sense of balance is necessary. It is useless to be dogmatic, to disregard the Communist point of view, or to assume that any solution offered is capable of quick fulfilment, or will not suffer many set-backs and disappointments.

In dealing with a subject of this magnitude the only possible method of approach is to state the principles which should govern the course of action recommended and to amplify these principles by means of a few examples.

The most suitable approach is to consider what are regarded as the four main aspects of the matter: The time factor—Armaments reduction—Avoidance of foolish and unsuccessful enterprises—Reasonable compromise.

It does not seem that these principles, or their application, are affected in any way by Marshal Stalin's death. There are signs of a better atmosphere and it may be that eventually we shall find that the change in leadership has altered East–West relations for the better; but final judgment on this point must await events, which may not take shape for many months.

TIME

War in Korea and Indo-China, guerrilla operations in Malaya and parts of Africa, subversive activities and propaganda on a great scale almost everywhere, with the whole process backed by immense fleets, armies and air forces, poised for instant action, and equipped with atomic weapons. These are conditions which we obviously cannot solve, or to any noticeable extent mitigate, except by long and patient processes.

History provides ample evidence that prolonged abuse and hatred cannot be converted quickly into enduring friendship. Spain and England were temporarily reconciled by the marriage of Philip II and Mary, but the reconciliation did not outlive Mary's death. It took America a long time to forget George III and the "Red Coats". The agreement signed between Germany and Russia immediately before the outbreak of war in 1939 did not—in spite of the similarity of the two systems of government—result in even a cursory friendship, and did not prevent Hitler attacking Russia 2 years later. The partition of India in 1947 revealed very quickly—in a terrible form, resulting in death and disaster to many hundreds of thousands—the age-long feud between Muslim and Hindu.

Most of the comparatively minor differences of creed, race and ideas are, however, being gradually reconciled; but it has been a long and tedious process and the end is not yet in sight. It would be contrary to experience if the even more bitter, and global, hostility between Democracy and Communism could be reconciled, except over a period of many years, perhaps many decades or even generations.

We must, therefore, accept the fact that the present world disturbance will take a long time to remedy.

ARMAMENTS

Although it is true that the ultimate salvation of the world depends on spiritual and moral values, it is apparent that under present conditions they are by no means the only considerations. Both East and West are heavily armed. In some places their forces are actually in action; but in most they are used to threaten, or to counter a real or imaginary threat by the other side.

In January last a distinguished team of B.B.C. experts in the programme "Any Questions?" were asked what was the main asset possessed by the Free World in its struggle against Communism. They replied* with a list of platitudes in which a number of moral values were enumerated—Christian principles, belief in ourselves, courage, integrity, and others. Not one member of the team mentioned anything of a material nature. Czechoslovakia in 1939 and again in 1948, Norway, Denmark and Holland in 1940, all possessed high spiritual and moral values, but these did not save them from their enemies who took a more realistic and practical view of affairs. Mahatma Gandhi relied solely on moral values to gain his ends; but

* Replies given are, of course, entirely impromptu, and not considered replies.

HOW WILL IT END?

it was the British–Indian armies which prevented a Japanese invasion of India. The British withdrawal from India was brought about not by Gandhi's faith, but by material considerations. We were just not prepared to provide on a permanent, or semi-permanent, basis the large British garrison which Lord Wavell, the Commander-in-Chief, considered necessary for the maintenance of law and order.

Without doubt moral values of the kind listed by the B.B.C. team will play a great part in solving our problems; but it is very dangerous to give the impression that material matters are of little, or no, consequence. Sir Winston Churchill—whose opinion is of some value in these matters—thinks that America's possession of the atom bomb has played a great part in preserving Western freedom. Our opponents are also very practical people. One cannot forget the remark attributed to Marshal Stalin when at a high-level conference during the war the advantage of having the support of the Pope was emphasized. His only contribution to the discussion was the question "The Pope —and how many divisions has he got?"

A proper perspective is essential in this matter. Without high regard for moral values no cause can prosper permanently; but the adage that "God helps those who help themselves" is a very true one in international affairs in the 1950s.

We must solve our problems by a proper blend of moral and material values. We will not solve them by too much emphasis on one to the detriment of the other.

Although we may not think a Third World War is likely the fact remains that both East and West consider a certain minimum, and a very high and costly minimum, of armed strength is absolutely essential to their safety and security. Obviously this great array of troops, armed with the most formidable weapons, almost deployed for battle and in close proximity, is itself a danger to peace, as well as being a crushing burden on world economy.

Yet, in the present temper of the nations, the practical difficulties of getting agreement, on even a modest measure of mutual disarmament, seem almost insuperable. Goodwill is so lacking, and suspicion so great, that no scheme is acceptable without rigid guarantees of good faith—which in practice means inspection, covering civil, as well as military, establishments. In the vast areas involved—practically the whole land-mass of the world—it appears impossible to devise a system of inspection sufficiently watertight to satisfy either West or East.

It is difficult to avoid the conclusion that for a long time to come a high proportion of world effort will be devoted to the production of war equipment and that our sons, and some of our daughters—and perhaps their sons and daughters—are destined to be trained to arms. The effect of war production, and training, on future generations cannot be foreseen. We have only experienced it for a short time; but it is possible that after several decades—when nobody can remember the time when preparation for war was not the main activity of man—it may produce unexpected, and perhaps startling, changes in the character and general make-up of the human race.

We can be quite certain that any scheme of general disarmament on a large scale is most unlikely in the near future. Relief can only come over a period of years.

Nothing Succeeds Like Success

During the war years the Allied powers made few plans beyond the defeat of Germany and Japan. America and Britain—particularly President Roosevelt—considered that a reasonable post-war settlement with Russia was attainable. The Soviet thought otherwise and regarded the war as merely a stage, or incident, in the march of Communism. Russia ended the war with a clear-cut plan to take advantage of chaotic conditions to promote World Communism. The Free World had no plans for combating this and was consequently at a marked disadvantage. Under these circumstances some mistakes were to be expected.

Many of these mistakes have, however, been very expensive and it is important that we should avoid similar errors in future. The following are a few of the difficult situations which Democracy has created, or acquiesced in, to her detriment.

Loss of initiative

For a long time we were content to allow the Soviet almost complete monopoly in propaganda. Russia maintained her war-time forces: we and our friends disbanded much of ours.

The Berlin "Island"

The administration of West Berlin would be difficult even with goodwill on all sides. Positioned as it is in the Soviet Sector, and surrounded by those whose sole aim was to inconvenience the Democratic powers, it has been a constant source of friction and worry.

HOW WILL IT END?

The Veto in the Security Council of U.N.O.

This is a one-sided rule which operates greatly to the advantage of the Soviet.

The war in Korea

This campaign has at least demonstrated that the Democratic nations are prepared to go to great lengths to uphold the principles, and prestige, of U.N.O. We cannot doubt the high-minded resolve which promoted the decision to intervene in Korea; but apart from this salve to our consciences it has brought us nothing but tribulation. America alone has suffered nearly 170,000 casualties (up to January, 1953) in Korea. Many fine divisions of American and European troops, a numerous fleet and a great air-force, are engaged in this remote part of Asia while Europe—the decisive area in the struggle between East and West—is still inadequately garrisoned. Against our forces in Korea hardly a single Russian fighting man, and not a very great amount of Russian-made equipment, is deployed. In addition the campaign has been a bad advertisement for U.N.O. The unfortunate Koreans have had the rake of war dragged up and down their country for nearly 3 years. All semblance of normal Government and life has been destroyed: only starvation, disease and misery exist. If this is the price of liberation we shall not in future find many people who want to be liberated.

In spite of the good intentions the price of the Korean campaign has been a very heavy one. We cannot afford another of the same kind.

Recognition of the Pekin Government

To many this premature recognition was a great mistake. It not only put us out of step with America; but, to use Lord Vansittart's words " . . . rendered negotiation impossible by playing a trump card too soon without taking a trick."

The case of Spain

It is difficult to find good reasons for the hostility towards Spain shown by the Free World. It is true that her form of government is not one which we would choose for ourselves, but it is more akin to our way of thinking than those of Iron Curtain countries and is, after all, a matter for Spaniards to decide. The majority appear to like it; the country is more prosperous than it has been for generations; they do not attempt to force their ideas on others; against great pressure from Hitler they remained neutral during the war, and they conduct themselves in international affairs with a dignity, and degree of honesty, which others might follow with advantage. Yet Spain has been refused admission to U.N.O., and many leading men in this and other countries are adamant in their demands to deny to Spain what they willingly accord to Russia, Persia and others who make no effort to disguise their hostility to our own country and our friends.

The close cooperation of Spain with the Western Powers since 1945 would have resulted in a much stronger Western European defence to-day. The Free World is not so secure, nor has Western Europe such an abundance of friends, that they can afford to "cold shoulder", for purely academic reasons, a nation whose cooperation is so immensely to their advantage. The case of Spain is a good example of unbalanced thinking—a case of giving theory, and so-called moral values, an unjustified preponderance over practical considerations.

Abadan

It is probable that the Soviet had little hand in events which led to abandonment of the Anglo-Iranian Oil Company's property in Persia. It is, however, certain that the event gave her the greatest satisfaction. It is difficult to believe that this humiliating episode could not have been prevented if we had started to tackle the problem 12 or 18 months earlier.

These are a few examples of the manner in which the Democracies are frequently outwitted by their opponents. We seem to make a habit of getting ourselves into difficult situations—mainly through high-minded motives which often bear little relation to realities. These mistakes lower Democratic prestige throughout the world, and give the impression among "waverers" that we are no match for the Communists in tactics and acumen.

Success on the other hand is like a snowball. One success leads to others and eventually to victory.

REASONABLE COMPROMISE

The main tenet of Democracy is freedom—freedom to select one's own rulers; freedom to criticize by speech or pen; freedom to do anything we like provided we do not harm others unduly. Our laws and regulations are framed to give this freedom to all, and we only impose restrictions to safeguard the rights of others. We can do anything, provided it is not contrary to a set of laws which are in most countries meticulously defined and, on the whole, administered with common sense.

This being so we must be careful not to deny to our opponents those things which we claim as a right for ourselves. When we begin to examine this aspect of the problem it is at once apparent that although we could compromise with Communism on many matters which are in dispute it is necessary first to agree on certain principles which are fundamental to a solution of our differences. These principles can be very simply stated:

First. Each group must acknowledge the right of the other to live under its chosen form of government and in accordance with its own ideology—however alien and repugnant the practices and methods of the one may be to the other.

In other words we should agree to the principle—let us have our Democracy and you can have your Communism, a policy of peaceful coexistence.

Secondly. The Soviet must abandon her missionary tactics. We can never agree to her right to use *any means* to convert the whole world to Communism. They are at liberty to consolidate Communism within their own territories. Outside their own territories they have a perfect right to state the Communist case, and to further Communism by argument, and peaceful means, within the law of the countries concerned. We do not accept their right to do more than this.

By reducing the essentials to these two simple principles, the problem is greatly simplified, and we get clear of the welter of comparatively trivial matters which tend to obscure the issue. It must be agreed that this reduction of fundamentals means that we accept the fact that things which the Free World deplores and detests will go on in Communist countries—religious persecution, the secret police and the faked trials, purges and forced-labour camps. However, these are matters within the sovereignty of the Soviet countries. If we do not accept their right to conduct their affairs as they choose we weaken our own claim for similar treatment. While we can never approve the horrors which go on behind the Iron Curtain we must remember that the affairs of Democracy are not always conducted to perfection, or according to the high ideals which we profess. An unbiased critic could not have always approved religious intolerance in Ireland and India, the French method of conducting the recent elections in the Saar or the manner in which racial problems have been handled in South Africa.

Acceptance of these two principles also means that we must give up any drastic attempts to rescue minorities behind the Iron Curtain, or Satellite States which are nominally Communist, but which we believe have a majority of non-Communists. To many this would be a most distasteful decision; but knight-errantry of this kind has already worked to our disadvantage and has not infrequently been ill-conceived. Too often those we seek to rescue have no desire to be rescued: too often the price of liberation—as in Korea—must seem heavier than the original affliction. Together with Communist missionary tactics it is perhaps the greatest source of friction to-day. Neither have a place under a policy of peaceful coexistence.

The next stage is to formulate, in outline, definite proposals for easing, and eventually stopping, the process which has been defined in this book as "*The New Warfare*".

It is here that Marshal Stalin's death may have some repercussions. We do not know what policy Mr. Malenkov and his associates will pursue, or whether he will be able to maintain the stability of government and continuity of policy which characterized his predecessor's regime. The leaders of the Free World, whilst ready to respond, may, with good reason, hesitate to enter into serious discussions on basic problems until they have got the measure of the new regime and are able to judge its stability. Nevertheless, the changed conditions afford an opportunity for a new approach which should not be missed.

The approach, when made, and subsequent action, might be attempted in four stages:

Stage I

An early meeting at the very highest level between representatives of America, Britain and Russia—and possibly Communist China*—with the object of attaining agreement on the two principles enumerated above.

This will obviously be the most critical stage, and most difficult fence to surmount.

Stage II

Stage I to be followed by discussions, and examination, in every locality and sphere, where there is dispute and tension between West

---

* Desirable as it may be there are obvious difficulties in bringing Communist China into the discussions, so long as she remains unrepresented on U.N.O., and her government recognized by Britain but not by the U.S.A.

HOW WILL IT END?

and East. In some matters—such as the Korean War, the Austrian Peace Treaty, relations between East and West Germany and tension in the councils of U.N.O.—these would have to be at a very high level. In smaller matters—such as control of propaganda in certain areas, traffic control in and out of Berlin, shipping in the Baltic, etc.—discussion could be on a local basis.

This stage might be a lengthy one, and complete success everywhere is not to be expected.

Stage III

As soon as a reasonable measure of success in Stage II had been achieved, what might be termed a period of tranquillity, for the consolidation of better behaviour and relations, might start.

Stages II and III would probably overlap without any definite date for terminating the former and beginning the latter. The duration of Stage III cannot be determined in advance: it might go on for years.

Stage IV

Further approaches. These might take the form of another conference at the highest level. By this time, if all had gone reasonably well, an atmosphere might have been created in which useful discussions for mutual disarmament, on a worth-while scale, would be profitable.

This is as far as we can go.

It is not claimed that these proposals would all succeed or that they are even practicable in their entirety. Any road leading to better understanding is certain to be a long and difficult one. It will obviously not be easy to get agreement among the Free World nations to adopt a common policy towards the Soviet—a disability from which the latter does not suffer, in view of her dominant position in the Communist World.

It is merely claimed that the suggestions are the basis of a plan— and a plan is what the Free World lacks in its handling of International affairs under post-war conditions.

This plan is based, not on spectacular, or immediate, results brought about by some master-stroke of wizardry—which is impracticable and certain to fail—but by a methodical and long-term process which may have some chance of success.

The aim is to produce, eventually, world conditions in which all men can live—not in complete agreement, which is impossible- -but in reasonable accord, without the fear of devastating war and without the crushing economic burden which preparation for total war entails.

It will be apparent that the above proposals, or any others for improving world relations, may fail. Indeed, experience over the past 5 or 6 years gives the impression that the chances of success are remote. It is satisfactory, however, to record that Mr. Malenkov, in his address at Marshal Stalin's funeral, emphasized the Soviets desire for peace. It would be wrong not to respond to this frame of mind and the less provocative attitude recently adopted by the East.

To the logical and fair minded, with a definite urge for a peaceful settlement, the principle of peaceful coexistence seems so utterly reasonable and sensible. It is also thoroughly practical as both world groups possess self-sufficient economies. We must strive hard, and if necessary long, to achieve success. If in the end we fail, or are not immediately successful, what course is the Free World to follow?

The answer is clear.

First. We must fight every aspect of "The New Warfare", with skill and determination.

Secondly. We must be ready to fight, and win, a Third World War, of the shooting kind, if it comes about. We must be prepared to win quickly, in order to prevent world chaos which would result from a prolonged struggle.

Thirdly. We must make clear that we are ready, at any time, to negotiate with the immediate object of improving relations, and the ultimate aim of a settlement based on the principle of "peaceful coexistance", as outlined above.

EPILOGUE

It has been the purpose of this book to state the facts of what is termed "*The New Warfare*", and to offer suggestions which might bring about a gradual improvement in international relations.

In doing this I have emphasized the importance of compromise, to a degree which some may think goes too far, and savours of appeasement.

I have, however, been at pains to qualify this by enumerating certain principles on which Democracy must take its stand and in defence of which the Free World must be prepared for *any* eventuality. These are matters which we regard as more important than life itself. To use President Eisenhower's words in his inaugural address on the 20th January, 1953:

" ... For in the final choice a soldier's pack is not so heavy a burden as a prisoner's chains. ..."

To some it may seem that the more friendly attitude of the Soviet in recent weeks paves the way for a speedy easement of world tension and a quick solution to all our problems. I cannot accept this view. The differences in ideology are too great, and the hostility and insults have gone on for too long, to be resolved in a period calculated in weeks or months. Nevertheless, the germ of some degree of reconciliation, based on peaceful coexistence, exists.

Now, perhaps more than ever in the history of the world, is the time for statesmanship, and a time when every word affecting our problems—written or spoken —should be weighed and calculated in a responsible manner.

C. N. B.